WHAT PEOPLE ARE SAYING ABOUT
Growing Up Ziglar

"No one can tell you who you are. It doesn't matter who your parents are or where you come from; you're the only one who gets to decide who you're going to be. Few people can demonstrate that better than Julie Ziglar Norman. The daughter of one of America's most well-known and loved motivators, Julie found God where most of us do: somewhere in between the lofty ideal we're told about and the big mess we often make of our lives."

—DAVE RAMSEY, *New York Times* best-selling author
and nationally syndicated radio host

"Julie Ziglar Norman continues the family legacy of sharing answers for those who are searching for the truth. In *Growing Up Ziglar: A D‒‒‒‒ ‒ Broken Path from Heartache to Hope*, Julie's own search for truth wil‖ and enlighten you. Her hard-earned words contain a clarity and ‖ that are surely welcome in today's world."

—ANDY ANDREWS, *New York Times* best-selling
of *The Noticer* and *The Traveler's Gift*

"Julie has truly lived EVERY WOMAN'S story. What she shares is r‹ What she reveals is real truth. What she offers is real freedor‖ CANNOT walk away with just one—it is a book that MUST be gifte‹ of the women in your life!"

—KATHLEEN D. MAILER, Founder/Editor-in-Chief
of *Today's Businesswoman Magazine* and author of *Prepare to Prosper: Taking Your Business to a Higher Level*

"Julie Ziglar Norman's masterful memoir will take you on a journey beneath the surface and underneath the shadow of her famous father's larger-than-life persona. With frank honesty, her story shows the love and support she found there, as well as the pressure she spent her life trying to ease. Her personal revelations will not only allow you to see inside the Ziglar family but will give you insight into your own. You'll leave these pages and Julie's story with a clearer view of yourself, your loved ones, and, most importantly, your God."

—PRISCILLA SHIRER, Bible teacher and author

"In this extremely raw and transparent recording of the powerful story of experience and lessons of Julie Ziglar Norman, you will see that deep down, we all go through valleys. I rarely endorse books, but because I truly believe that many will be transformed through this one...I say... read it."

—NICK VUJICIC, motivational speaker and founder of Life Without Limbs

"There's nothing like living in that sweet place of God's grace, mercy, and love, escaping our self-imposed prison of regret and shame. Julie Ziglar Norman's brave testimony shines with the magnificent light of God, a light that seems to burn brighter with every chapter she writes and every personal error of judgment she reveals. God is more efficient in the restore and renew process than any counselor or friend could possibly be, though He may use a counselor or friend along the way. There's been no book that describes that process as succinctly as *Growing up Ziglar: A Daughter's Broken Path from Heartache to Hope*. Thank you, Julie!"

—REBECCA SNELL, Cofounder of The Bonded Family

"Transparency and humility are incredibly refreshing gifts—to the one exuding them as well as those witnessing them. A companionship, great hope, and comforting peace are experienced on both sides, in a way that offers palpable healing. Through the pages of *Growing Up Ziglar* you're sure to fall in love with, and have great respect for, Julie Ziglar Norman. Better still, as I'm certain is her reason for writing this book, no matter your past choices or current circumstances, you'll be inspired to make the right choices and be the best you!"

—DENISE TAYLOR, author of *Heavenly Birth: A Mother's Journey. A Daughter's Legacy*, inspirational speaker, and creator of the We GET To Foundation

"There are two axioms that Julie proves true in offering faith, hope, and love in *Growing Up Ziglar: A Daughter's Broken Path from Heartache to Hope*: 'A troubled faith is better than no faith at all' and 'Trouble handled rightly honors God.' Julie Ziglar Norman lives out both beautifully in this incredibly transparent story of God's grace and love. Every person who has ever fallen and failed will be encouraged to get back up and be their best after reading this book!"

—DR. DWIGHT "IKE" REIGHARD, Lead Pastor, Piedmont Church, www.PiedmontChurch.tv

"*Growing Up Ziglar: A Daughter's Broken Journey from Heartache to Hope* is the most honest, inspiring, and encouraging book you'll read this year. Its life lessons will make you laugh, cry, think, and soar!"

—DAVE ANDERSON, President of LearnToLead and author of *How to Lead by THE BOOK*

"*Growing Up Ziglar*...I have never read a book where the author was more transparent and willing to share the real journey of their life. Julie has opened a door for us to see how the love of God can heal and transform the brokenness of our hearts and lives. I wept at the pain and laughed out loud at her great sense of humor. I believe that this book is a beautiful example that can encourage women to discover that they can live free of shame and truly be forgiven. Thank you, Julie, for sharing your incredible heart with the world."

—MARY A. MICHEL, CEO/Founder of Journey
of the Heart Ministries/Center of Hope
www.journeyoftheheart.org

"Once in a great while a book comes along that not only touches your heart but also pierces the soul. *Growing Up Ziglar* is such a book. Julie Ziglar Norman opens her life to public view, and the result is a powerful, inspiring, and nurturing adventure of faith. Every woman should read this book!"

—TONY JEARY, executive coach and author
of *Strategic Acceleration*

"Julie Ziglar Norman is a personal friend of mine and a precious person refined by the very grace and power of God into His image. While the great motivator, Zig Ziglar, is her daddy, Jesus Christ is her Father. This book tells the story of how both have helped shape her life. Her story will touch your heart and soothe your soul, leaving you with complete confidence that God is loving and forgiving and that He can and will heal those who seek Him."

—BETH CHAPMAN, Alabama's 51st Secretary of State

"Practical, honest, powerful! This is a *very* good book. The insights of Julie Ziglar Norman are an empowering dose of genuine responsibility and truth for all believers. Readers will be challenged to move through personal facades toward the bedrock of what separates us from Christ. Then each is encouraged to choose His freedom."

—KIM MEEDER, Founder of Crystal Peaks Youth
Ranch, best-selling author, and speaker

"Julie Ziglar's book *Growing Up Ziglar* is a first-person testimonial to the redemption and restoration our great God gives to His children through all the experiences of our lives. This book is for everyone, and especially for women who have made choices they regret and wondered if they could ever be free from the pain of those decisions. Julie's own experience points us to a God who lives to forgive and heal—everything."

—MELINDA DELAHOYDE, President of CareNet

"Julie Ziglar Norman's *Growing Up Ziglar* could easily be called *Trans-Parent* or *Confessions of a Successful Christian*. Those who read this masterpiece will realize that being successful includes sin, struggles, and strife. Failing is just part of L.I.F.E. and Julie's transparency will stun you, startle you, and strengthen you. In an era where authenticity, originality, and being transparent are preached but not always practiced, Julie's book unveils the truth in a tell-all fashion that will surprise you. Prepare to read cover to cover with your mouth wide open!"

—MICHAEL J. MAHER, Founder of The Generosity
Generation and national best-selling author of
((7L)) *The Seven Levels of Communication.*

JULIE ZIGLAR NORMAN

GROWING UP ZIGLAR

A DAUGHTER'S BROKEN JOURNEY
from HEARTACHE *to* HOPE

Guideposts
New York, New York

Growing Up Ziglar

ISBN: 978-0-8249-4531-2

Published by Guideposts
16 East 34th Street
New York, NY 10016
Guideposts.org

Copyright © 2012 by Julie Ziglar Norman. All rights reserved.

This book, or parts thereof, may not be reproduced, stored in a retrieval system, or transmitted in any form or by any means, electronic, mechanical, photocopying, recording or otherwise, without the written permission of the publisher.

Distributed by Ideals Publications, a Guideposts company
2630 Elm Hill Pike, Suite 100
Nashville, TN 37214

Guideposts and *Ideals* are registered trademarks of Guideposts.

Scripture references are from the following sources: The Holy Bible, King James Version (kjv). The Holy Bible, American Standard Version (asv).The Holy Bible, New International Version®, niv®. Copyright © 1973, 1978, 1984 by Biblica, Inc.™ Used by permission of Zondervan. All rights reserved worldwide. The Holy Bible, New King James Version (nkjv). Copyright © 1997, 1990, 1985, 1983, 1982 by Thomas Nelson, Inc. Used by permission. The New American Standard Bible® (nasb), copyright © 1960, 1962, 1963, 1968, 1971, 1972, 1973, 1975, 1977, 1995 by The Lockman Foundation. Used by permission. The Holy Bible, English Standard Version® (esv), copyright © 2001 by Crossway Bibles, a publishing ministry of Good News Publishers. Used by permission. All rights reserved.

Every attempt has been made to credit the sources of copyrighted material used in this book. If any such acknowledgment has been inadvertently omitted or miscredited, receipt of such information would be appreciated.

Cover design by Christopher Gilbert, Studio Gearbox
Cover photograph by Jean Ziglar
Interior design by Müllerhaus
Typeset by Müllerhaus

Printed and bound in the United States of America

CONTENTS

INTRODUCTION

For over a quarter of a century I lived every day with regret, shame, guilt, grief, pain, and a deep, underlying depression. I was exhausted from hurting and tired of running from the memory and magnitude of what I'd done and the life I'd been living. As the daughter of the motivator's motivator, Zig Ziglar, I knew that I needed to be positive and that "negative thinking" would just make things worse.

So I gathered up all of my negative self-talk—the disgust, self-loathing, anger, bitterness, resentment, guilt, and shame—and squashed it down deep inside where it couldn't seep out and ruin the bright and practiced smile I presented to the world.

My thought life was like a war zone. The negative, self-degrading words that dominated my thinking battled daily with the positive, uplifting words of encouragement my father taught from the platform and in his many books. One thing I knew for sure, I was positive I was miserable!

Many people know a little something about my father being a motivational and inspirational icon, and they don't expect a child who had the obvious advantages of growing up with a loving, positive, encouraging father and mother to have made such a mess of her life. My double life as a secret misfit and an outward overachiever was a living lie, but it has led me to a life of transparency and the topics of repentance, restoration, and becoming your best you. My parents fully support my transparency, and their unwavering love for me is a blessing I thank God for daily.

For most of my life I heard my father say, "You have to be the right kind of person to succeed in life. You have to be before you can do. You have to do before you can have." I didn't understand what it meant to BE the "RIGHT KIND" of person until I was well into my fourth decade of living. Today I know that it is impossible to fully achieve what my father teaches without surrendering your life to God. It is only through God's power that man can overcome his selfish, self-destructive ways and become someone who can glorify God and praise Him in all things.

More than anything I want to help people who struggle with feeling that they can't come to Jesus until they become perfect. The notion that you have to be good and make all the right choices to be loved by God keeps countless numbers of people from the most astounding, uplifting, incredible relationship available to mankind. I didn't understand grace when I was first saved, and when I fell back into sin I thought Jesus would never have me back because I betrayed Him and let Him down. Now I know the sweetness of complete surrender, and I want everybody to know Jesus on that level.

The readers with whom I hope to resonate intuitively

"know" that God is the answer to their problems, but they feel unworthy of Him because they don't understand His grace. Some have never been to church, others have given up on going to church where they feel the absolute worst of all, but many are sitting in churches feeling less than, apart from, and undeserving of a relationship with Jesus and those who sit around them. They have prayed for forgiveness and rededicated their lives to Jesus innumerable times, and yet they are stuck, feeling unforgiven and unworthy of His love. So they exercise their freedom of choice and do another "this will make me feel better" compulsive behavior. I have firsthand knowledge that this tentative, one step forward and two steps back Christianity leads to fence-straddling misery.

The purpose I feel God has given me is found in 2 Corinthians 1:3–4: "Blessed be the God and Father of our Lord Jesus Christ, the Father of mercies and God of all comfort, who comforts us in all our tribulation, that we may be able to comfort those who are in any trouble, with the comfort with which we ourselves are comforted by God" (NKJV).

I believe God wants me to be completely transparent so that I can comfort others with the same comfort that God has extended to me. It is my prayer that what I share with you in this book will encourage you to know God, to serve and live for Him in ways you never thought possible—ways that are not possible without a deep and abiding relationship with Him. My heart is for you to KNOW HIM!

CHAPTER ONE

AVAILABLE, WILLING, AND OBEDIENT

THE COMMAND I COULDN'T IGNORE

That hot Sunday morning in the waning days of the summer of 2005 started out like so many others. Six years earlier, my husband, Jim, and I had moved from the bustling suburbs of the Dallas/Ft. Worth Metroplex to the sleepy little town of Alvord, Texas. It had taken some time and lots of visiting, but we'd found a church we loved, and we treasured all thirty of the regular attendees. We enjoyed knowing, *really knowing*, everyone in the fellowship, so it didn't seem unusual when my friend Missy pulled me aside as soon as we walked into the church foyer.

It *was* unusual when Missy began telling me about a dream she'd had the night before. Our church would be considered conservative by most, and what I was about to hear was not an ordinary discussion—even among our most colorful attendees!—

but I was riveted in place because I'd just that very week finished a personal Bible study about God speaking to people through dreams in biblical times.

Missy said she didn't know what the dream meant, but it was made clear in her dream that she was to tell me, "You are to do the thing you've been asked to do, and God can't use you fully until you've done it."

I could feel my heart pounding, and it seemed to beat faster with every word Missy spoke. I knew immediately to what she was referring, and with an inward groan I recalled the terse conversation with my sister and my refusal to even consider her unthinkable request. I thanked Missy for telling me and assured her I understood what her dream meant...but I wasn't about to tell her any of the sordid details. A distinct feeling of impending doom washed over me. The doors were about to be flung wide open on the very thing I'd been secretly dreading for over a quarter of a century. Vivid, unwelcome memories crowded in as my practiced denial fell by the wayside. My past had finally caught up with me.

I'm Positive I'm Miserable

It is hard for some people to believe that a daughter of motivational icon Zig Ziglar and his famous "Redhead," Jean Abernathy Ziglar, would have any problems at all. People ask me all the time what it was like "growing up Ziglar." Then they launch into guessing how it might have been growing up with the world's greatest motivator for a father. They don't realize that the daddy I grew up with was a traveling salesman. I'll admit, he was an extremely optimistic, happy, enthusiastic salesman, and he was teaching positive thinking (at home and in the sales field) by the time I was a teenager, but he was not famous or even very well known on the national level until I was about eighteen years old.

In our family home, negative words like *stupid, dumb, idiot,* and *hate,* or any hurtful combination of words, were not allowed. I'm quite sure my little friends thought I was from a different planet when I'd say someone was "less than bright," or "not the sharpest knife in the drawer."

If I was sick and you asked how I felt, I wouldn't say I felt bad—no, I'd say I felt "less than good." If I sprained my wrist and you tried to comfort me, I'd tell you all about how grateful I was because a sprained wrist is so much better than a broken arm. Nothing got credit for being what it was, and negative attitudes were discussed and adjusted. While I am truly grateful that I learned how to minimize problems instead of maximize them, when the bigger, tougher issues of life began to happen, I put them behind me so quickly I never fully processed or even acknowledged what had happened. I just moved on and hoped for the best.

I was taught to look for the good in everything, but trying to find a way to express negative feelings with positive words could get pretty frustrating at times. It was in one of those moments during my teen years that I proclaimed I would one day write a book titled *I'm Positive I'm Miserable.* I had no way of knowing that

I'd ultimately have more than enough material to fill several volumes under that title.

When Dad's speaking career began to take off, it took off in a big way, especially in our hometown of Dallas, Texas, thanks in large part to the endorsement and support of the late Mary Kay Ash of Mary Kay Cosmetics. When Dad's notoriety increased, I became acutely aware of trying to protect his public image. I had a lot of challenges as a teenager and young adult, and I realized I was making choices that weren't consistent with what Dad was teaching. I never wanted to cause him embarrassment, so I did my best to keep people from finding out he was my father. When that wasn't possible, I found myself living life with two faces. On the outside I was positive. On the inside I was miserable.

By the time my friend Missy told me about her dream, I was fifty years old and at a point in life where I had made great progress toward being more positive than miserable—at least in the areas I was willing to face. I shouldn't have been surprised that God wanted me to dig into my past and deal with the hurts and shame that survived just below the everyday level of consciousness. I had experienced firsthand that God didn't want me to settle for less than His best in my relationships. I was about to learn the full extent of God's handiwork, the intricate details that had been set in motion years before, and the length to which He would go to draw me into an intimate relationship with Him.

THE EDITOR

Full circle, as I understand it, is when you find yourself back at the starting place and realize that a seemingly insignificant act or incident profoundly altered the course of your life. Until my life went full circle, I had no idea what made me decide to enter the *Guideposts* Writers Workshop Contest in 1992. I grew up reading the little spiritual magazine of encouragement that the late Dr. Norman Vincent Peale and his late wife, Ruth Stafford Peale, started in 1945. After I left home, my mother gave me a subscription of my own every year for Christmas—a wonderful tradition she continues to this very day.

Through the years I often poured over the announcement about entering the biannual Guideposts Writers Workshop Contest, so I knew winners went to Rye, New York, for a week of intensive training on how to write an inspirational story. I also knew that I'd had a *Guideposts*-type experience on my job at Ross Downs, the Thoroughbred training track where I worked in the mideighties. I sent my story in just before the deadline and completely forgot about it until I received a letter stating that I had been chosen as one of the fifteen winners that year. I was stunned. Though I had entered, I had no expectations of winning, and my disbelief demanded I reread the letter several times before I called my husband to share the good news.

The workshop experience was electrifying. I learned volumes about inspirational writing in that short space of time, but it was an offhand remark and the explanation that followed that would dictate the next two decades of my life. Elizabeth and John Sherrill, best-selling coauthors of Corrie ten Boom's *The Hiding Place* and Pastor David Wilkerson's *The Cross and the Switchblade,* as well as longtime roving editors for *Guideposts* magazine, happened to be two of my writers' workshop teachers. They both commented that I was a natural editor, and the discussion that followed went into depth about what makes a good editor good. When I got back to Texas, I relayed to my dad all the high points of the trip, and as an afterthought, I told him what the Sherrills had said about my editing skills.

Dad said the news about my editing ability was particularly interesting information since he just happened to need an editor for his next book, *Over the Top*! I started working for Dad immediately, and over the next twenty years I edited or revised twenty-seven of my father's thirty books. In 2009 we coauthored *Embrace the Struggle: Living Life on Life's Terms.* The circumstances surrounding that book changed all of our lives.

THE FALL

Alarm is what I felt when I saw my parents' phone number light up the caller ID screen at 10:30 p.m. on March 7, 2007. They never called us that late. Sure enough, Mom's strained voice confirmed my fears, and I began pulling on clothes as she filled me in on the details. Dad had fallen down the entire length of the staircase in their home. He hit his head on the marble floor and then slammed headfirst into the front door. He'd been knocked out cold but regained consciousness shortly after the paramedics arrived. Mom said Dad was being taken by ambulance to the local hospital. I told her I was on the way, and within a matter of minutes I'd pulled out of my garage to begin the seventy-five-mile trip to the hospital.

When I arrived, I discovered my mother on a gurney in the emergency room hallway. THAT was not what I expected! The stress of the situation had caused Mom's heart to race out of control, and she'd become a patient herself. She told me my sister Cindy was in the examining room with Daddy and that they were waiting on the results of his CT scan. At the very least they expected to hold Dad overnight for observation. Mom had been given medication to slow her heart rate, and she was supposed to stay quiet and as calm as possible until it had a chance to work.

Within a few hours we had the bad news. Dad had two brain bleeds, and the next several hours would reveal the rest of the story. Mom's heart wasn't responding to the medication, and they were keeping her overnight as well. So, with the exception of my younger brother Tom—who was on vacation and trying to get back to Dallas as quickly as possible—there we were, shaking our heads at how quickly life can change.

My sister and I kept a close watch over Mom and Dad all night. Fortunately, the observation rooms had an adjoining door so Cindy and I switched rooms occasionally so we could each assess how we thought our parents were responding to their treatment.

Within a dozen hours Dad started repeating himself. His short-term memory was obviously affected, but we weren't too concerned. We'd seen that exact behavior when I'd had a serious concussion several years earlier, and my repetitiveness cleared up completely after three or four days.

By midmorning Mom's heart rate had returned to normal and she was released. Dad, however, was admitted to the hospital, and it was apparent he would be staying awhile. Overnight he'd developed vertigo, and the short-term memory loss was substantial. His brain bleeds and the potential for brain swelling had to be monitored closely.

Dad's biggest concern was what he'd do about upcoming speaking engagements if the doctor wouldn't release him from the hospital. He said he felt fine and was ready to go home, but it was obvious—at least for the moment—that Dad wouldn't be able to give one-, two-, or three-hour-long speeches, much less eight-hour talks like he had in the past. At times his memory was shorter than three minutes long. If something didn't change, and change quickly, we knew Dad's speaking career might be over.

My brother Tom, who is the CEO of our family-owned business, made it to the hospital and immediately canceled Dad's speaking engagements for the following week. When Tom explained Dad's short-term memory loss and his vertigo as the reasons for the cancellations, Peter Lowe, the owner of the Get Motivated Seminars where Dad spoke regularly, wisely suggested that possibly Dad could make future engagements by sitting down and using an interview format.

Dad was released from the hospital a few days later, and the doctors told him to take a "wait and see" attitude. Sometimes, as the brain heals, the swelling goes down and the memory improves; sometimes it doesn't. In Dad's case there was no improvement, but there was no keeping him off the road either. Dad totally embraced the idea of having Peter interview him onstage.

Peter did the first few interviews, then Tom asked either Krish Dhanam or Bryan Flanagan to accompany Dad onstage. Krish and Bryan are wonderful speakers in their own right who have both worked with our company for years and know Dad's material very well.

Four months later, at Dad's final "Born to Win Seminar," a self-improvement training event that he'd put on in Dallas for several decades, our family ended the seminar by telling our favorite stories about Daddy. Jay Hellwig, the husband of our top salesperson, noticed that the crowd was particularly responsive to the stories I told about Daddy and the interaction we had. Jay said it was obvious that I would be the best person to interview my father onstage. I had no idea that both Bryan and Krish struggled mightily when they had to interrupt and redirect Dad during an interview. He'd been their boss for so many years and they esteemed him so highly, it felt disrespectful to interrupt him. In their desire to help Dad, our company, and our family, they did as we asked without complaint, but when Jay made his suggestion, everyone readily agreed it would be a good solution.

The very next week my brother asked me if I would be willing to interview Dad at the big Get Motivated Seminars. I didn't hesitate when I said yes. I didn't stop to question if I might get nervous or if I could even speak in front of huge auditoriums full of people. I didn't consider if I would like a job that took me out of town over thirty weeks of the year or if I could handle both the speaking assignments and my editing job. I had long ago made the decision that I would be available, willing, and obedient to do the things my heavenly Father put in front of me to be done.

The decision was simple for me because I had been blessed to learn from Pastor Gene Smith that I didn't have to go looking for my purpose or even wonder what it might be. He explained that God was quite big enough to put my purpose directly in front of me AND handle the details. All I had to do was be available, willing, and obedient, and accept the assignment. Of course, this assignment—as far out of my comfort zone as it was—could in no way compare to the anguished path that Missy's dream, almost two years earlier, had set before me.

CHAPTER TWO

I NEVER WANTED THIS!

THE ACCIDENTAL SPEAKER

Even though I wasn't particularly looking forward to being onstage, I was excited about being able to travel with my mom and dad to all of the speaking engagements. It had been my prayer for a few years that I would find a way to spend more time with them. After all, Dad was in his eighties and Mom wasn't far behind.

Every time Daddy asked when I was going to come see him, I'd ask him when he was going to quit writing books! Dad has a habit of signing "three-book deals," where he commits to deliver three books to the publisher in a predetermined amount of time. From the first moment I began editing for him, my life has been defined by book deadlines. The more Daddy wrote, the less time I had to go see him. Helping him onstage meant that I'd be editing his books on the road, but we'd get to have meals together, and spending that time with my parents was a big perk. That was the upside.

For me, there was also a definite downside. Never in my life had I considered being a public speaker. It simply hadn't crossed my mind. Dad was the speaker. Interviewing Dad on stage was just me helping him continue to do what he loved—encourage others—and nothing more...right?

THE SPEECH TEACHER

Actually, if I'd had any desire to become a speaker, it would have been squelched the first time I tried speaking. Back in the fall of 1970, when I was a sophomore at Richardson High School in Richardson, Texas, I thought it'd be fun to sign up for speech class and learn a little bit of what my dad did for a living. There were about twenty-five students in the class, and our teacher didn't waste any time getting us started.

The first speaking assignment, if I'm remembering this correctly, required us to speak for three minutes. I don't recall what the topic was, but I do remember that several students spoke before I did. The quality of performances varied from great to awful. Some went over the time limit; some went under the time limit. One guy froze and had trouble getting out his first line. With relief I finished my speech, confident that I had stopped talking right on the three-minute mark, hadn't stuttered, mispronounced any words, or messed up in any discernible way.

At the next speech class our teacher returned our handwritten speeches with the grades boldly written in red and circled at the top of the page. As she handed them out, she'd call a name and announce the grade: "Barbara Green, A; Jill Williams, A-plus; Robbie Mathis, B-plus."

I was getting excited because I knew I'd done better than some of the people who were getting As. Then the teacher's voice rang out: "Julie Ziglar, C-minus." I was in shock, and even my classmates were stunned. Hanging jaws and wide, round eyes were proof of the level of disbelief that permeated the classroom. Even the guy who spoke only half of the allotted time got a higher grade than I did.

After class I waited for everyone to leave and told the teacher I didn't understand why she'd given me a C-minus. I said I thought I'd done well and I named a few people who had gotten higher grades but had fallen short in areas I did not. In my mind I can still see her sitting there at the desk, her hair pulled back into the tight bun she knotted up daily, lips tightly pursed. She adjusted her glasses, daintily cleared her throat, and said in a tone I'd never heard before and haven't heard since, "I happen to know who your father is, and I expect more from you!"

The teacher's little speech was not exactly what I would call motivational. I felt defeated before I'd even begun. I had done my best, and understood immediately that I was doomed! I don't know what made her think that the ability to get up in front of a room full of people and speak well was hereditary. I was only fifteen years old, and even I knew that wasn't how it worked!

The First Interview

Thirty-seven years spanned the time between my disastrous speech class and my first appearance with Dad on the big stage. It happened in Washington, DC, on Thursday, September 6, 2007. Hannah Newlin looked over her shoulder at me as she led my mom, dad, sister Cindy, and me to the green room in the Verizon Center.

"Would you like to take a look at the stage and see how the auditorium is set up so you'll know what to expect?" she asked.

Her question nearly threw me. I'd been trusting God and taking my thoughts captive since the minute I'd agreed to interview Dad on the Get Motivated platform. I was fully aware that eighteen thousand people were already in their seats and the majority of them had come specifically to see my father. I didn't need to look past the drawn black curtains to see them. I could hear their foot-stompin', hand-clapping, roaring cheers as they rooted for their pick in the dance contest for the free trip to Disney World. The very air in the Verizon Center was shaking with excitement, and I steadfastly held my thoughts in check. I refused to even imagine what it must look like from the stage. I knew in my heart I'd be fine, I'd be safe. God was in control—and I was with my daddy, after all. Nothing feels safer than being with your father, right?

Less than an hour later, Dad stepped up on that stage with me right behind him. Fireworks erupted all around us and Dad's

biggest fans jumped to their feet, clapping, whistling, and yelling, "We love you, Zig!" I helped Dad get settled in his seat and
started the introduction that I would make over one hundred
times in front of over one million people in the four years that
were to follow.

I'd take my seat next to Dad and start the interview with
the two most frequently asked questions: "How old is Zig now?"
and "Does he have any plans to retire?" We'd speak for twenty-
five minutes and we never covered the same thing twice! Dad
has so many stories and has taught on every topic from selling, to
marriage, to raising positive kids, to surviving grief and finding
Jesus. I never knew what might come up. I asked the same questions and was amazed at how many different answers applied.
Every once in a while, Dad would double back and start to repeat
himself; I would put my hand on his knee and say, "Dad, we've
already covered that one pretty thoroughly."

"I know that, Little One," Dad would reply, using his pet
name for me. Then he'd point out at the audience and quip, "But
I was watching and those two men right there in the second row
were not listening, so I thought I'd better say it again!" The audience would erupt in laughter, and Dad would wait patiently for
the laughter to die down a little, then he would say something to
the effect of, "I have a brilliant memory, it's just very short!" and
the crowd would roar with laughter again. Dad could always pull
it out of the hat with his quick wit.

STARTING WITH A BANG

Those first two weeks Dad and I spoke in front of more people than many speakers address in a lifetime! Between the Washington, DC, venue and two venues in Dallas, Texas, we appeared before over sixty thousand people. It was difficult for me to take it all in. One thing was for sure: none of it had anything to do with me, and I had done nothing to make it happen.

I started getting encouraging phone calls from friends when they found out I was speaking with Dad at the Get Motivated Seminars. The first call came from Marilyn Henderson, a good friend of mine from Tennessee. She was so excited when she called that I had a hard time understanding her at first. She told me that she got goose bumps when she read that I was speaking with my father. "God has been preparing you for this," Marilyn exclaimed. "You are ready!"

I was amazed and couldn't grasp the enormity of what she said. No matter what Marilyn stated, I had a comeback or excuse for why that couldn't be so. I wasn't really speaking; I was interviewing Dad, and that was a lot different than giving a speech. And my top-of-the-list reason? I didn't want this to be my future...when Dad didn't need my help anymore, I would be done with speaking. I would be done with editing and writing. At last I would get to be "Super Mammaw" to my twelve grandchildren. That had long been my plan for when Dad quit writing.

Finally, Marilyn announced, "Mark my words. You will be carrying your father's legacy forward. Mark my words."

With a degree of trepidation, I hid her words in my heart and watched tentatively for signs that Marilyn could be right. I really struggled to believe what she said...after all, I knew where I came from and what secrets lay buried there. My past was nothing like my father's.

CHAPTER THREE

JUST *BE*

୫୭

"WHY DIDN'T YOU TELL ME YOUR FATHER IS ZIG ZIGLAR?"

These days my last name is Norman, so I can go months—even years—before people discover who my father is. I prefer people get to know me before they do find out, in case that knowledge might skew their perception of me. Not that Dad's reputation would ever hurt me...I just don't want to be treated differently because of my father's fame.

I've actually had people I've known for a while get upset when they found out my father is Zig Ziglar. "Why didn't you tell me your father is Zig Ziglar?" they demand. "You didn't tell me who your daddy is," I retort. And then they say, "Yeah—but my daddy isn't Zig Ziglar!"

It hasn't always been that way. When my father was a pro-fessional salesman, nobody made much of a fuss over him. As far back as I can remember, Dad was always selling something. When I was very small I was unaware of the different products he sold, but I was aware of his travels. Daddy was often on the road from Monday morning until late Friday afternoon. On occasion, if he had a long way to drive to get to his territory, he'd even leave Sunday night so he could be ready to knock on doors first thing the next morning.

When Daddy was selling cookware, he used to take turns taking each one of his children on road trips with him. It was a great way for us to spend time with him individually, and— I found out recently—it allowed him to speak with the husband and wife while we played outside with their children. Dad has long taught that he most enjoys "two-fers"—two benefits for one effort. The kid entertainment system fit the bill perfectly!

THE FAULT IS MINE

I know you'll find this difficult to believe, but there are actually some people who might pick up a book authored by the child of a famous person hoping to get the scoop, the real truth, about the celebrity parent.

It seems that the more upright and good the parent is, the more the public wants to hear bad stuff told by angry, wounded children. But guess what? The blame falls on me. You won't hear any "dirt" from me; in fact, I well remember the day I knew that my dad could do *anything*!

I was about ten years old and I was cleaning my pet chipmunk's cage on the carport outside. I had put Chicker in a shoebox and set it on the roof of my mom's car to keep the dogs from sniffing around the box. I heard a funny *pop, pop, pop* noise, and turned around just in time to see the lid of that box pop off and watch helplessly as my chipmunk made a mad dash for freedom. I started yelling, "Daddy, Daddy, Chicker is loose! Get her, Daddy, get her!"

Daddy was just a few feet away washing his car, and when he heard my cries for help, he was on it! Suddenly my daddy took on the stature of a true superhero! He homed in on that chipmunk and immediately went into action! They zigged and they zagged, this way and that. Chicker would dart up a tree a little ways, and when Daddy got close she'd jump to the ground and they'd be off again. Over and over Daddy got close enough to grab the chipmunk, and she'd dart away again.

Fortunately, for Daddy and for me, our neighbors had louvered windows that happened to be open that day. Chicker ran up the side of their house, through the open window, and attached herself to the window screen. Daddy was able to reach in and grab her.

That's when things got really exciting! Immediately Daddy started yelling, "She's biting me! She's biting me! Hurry! Get me something to put her in!" I raced ahead of him back to the house and ran through the door hollerin' for something to put the chipmunk in. Mama grabbed an open, half-eaten box of vanilla wafers, and she ran to Dad as he cleared the door, holding the box out ahead of her.

Before Daddy slung that chipmunk into the box, I saw that Chicker had sunk her two front teeth clean through the fleshy underside of Dad's thumb. Blood was running clear down to his elbow and dripping onto the floor. But what really got my attention was the way my Daddy's fingers were curled around that chipmunk, holding her tightly enough that she couldn't escape even if she released her tooth hold and struggled to get away. I have often thought that God held onto me in much the same way.

My father has told me many times that he has never experienced anything more painful than having that chipmunk bite through his thumb. He has spoken often of how he had to resist the temptation to violently shake that chipmunk off his hand, and though he never said it, I bet he would have liked to stomp that chipmunk a time or two after it hit the ground. Daddy's character, his selfless desire to do the right thing for me, allowed him to get the chipmunk and save his daughter from some serious heartbreak. Daddy also got the never-ending adoration of his daughter.

Often when I speak, I ask the audience to raise their hands if any of the children they so lovingly and carefully raised went out and did exactly the very thing they warned them against doing. There is always a bit of nervous laughter before the vast majority of hands go up. I then explain that I am doing the disclaimer portion of my talk, and I tell them how I have wonderful parents, but I, of my own volition, made a lot of bad choices. I want everyone to know up front that there won't be a Zig Ziglar bashing session. My father is the right kind of person and he did his best by me; I'm the one who made my life a mess!

Sadly, from the age of thirteen to thirty that mess was so big I tried to keep it a secret that I was Zig Ziglar's daughter. I was tremendously proud of my father, and I was horribly ashamed of the choices I was making in my life that would embarrass him if he, or anyone who knew him, found out about them. The reason I was making bad choices was because I did not yet understand one of the most foundational principles my father was teaching: you have to BE before you can DO, and you have to DO before you can HAVE.

I was stuck at "BE." I believe I got stuck at "BE" because Dad raised me without the Instruction Manual. I am absolutely serious. Dad was a good father. He always gave it his best effort. He taught me to obey the law, tell the truth, and work hard, but he didn't become a Christian until I was a few weeks shy of being seventeen years old. Until then, Dad couldn't have known everything he needed to be teaching me.

I missed being raised in church. I missed being taught biblical principles and hearing Bible stories with morals. I missed being taught the importance of keeping yourself pure for marriage. I know God's Instruction Manual, the Bible, made all the difference in the life of my little brother Tom. Tom is almost ten years younger than I; Dad raised him with the Instruction Manual, took him to church, and read him Bible stories. Tom has had a totally different life than my sisters and I, and it is most apparent in the choices he has made. I believe it is because Tom learned the "why and how" behind the rules and expectations.

Dad teaches that you have to BE the right kind of person first. These days I absolutely love talking about being the right kind of person. Finally I understand what my father's saying means! I had to live through my twenties, thirties, and into my early forties before I began to catch on. Call me a slow learner, but every time I heard Dad say "you have to be the right kind of person," I thought... *and what is that? According to whose standards? What* DOES *that mean?*

I am sure he explained it many times, but I was so far from being able or willing to try to be the right kind of person that I couldn't get beyond the question of whose standards were being used to measure right and wrong.

I was stuck on my "rights" and it never occurred to me that certain life principles simply made life less complicated and easier to live. I was making a straightforward thing difficult because I was afraid I might be asked to change, do something hard, or give up something I enjoyed.

I used to congratulate myself on having an open mind. I have since learned that my mind was open by only a single, very narrow crack into which I wedged a thousand feeble excuses for not trying to be more than I already was, or the best I could be.

After so many years of being the "wrong kind" of person, I've discovered that when you are happy to "BE" you, when you know why you do what you do, and you feel confident that you know who you are, and *Whose* you are, that is joy unleashed! When you are free to be your best you—the right kind of person—you can look forward to the next day with eager anticipation instead of dread and fear. Sadly, it wasn't always this way for me.

IT'S A DECISION

I well remember the first time I came face to face with the fact that I could make a different choice and actively DO something to change my life, if only I would.

My mother actually brought this to light for me when I was in my late teens...and miserable. I called Mom on the phone to complain about my life AGAIN, when she suddenly interrupted me and said, "This is hard for me to say, but you need to know that I cannot listen to you talk about your problems anymore. When you become willing to do something to change your circumstances, let me know, and I'll support you any way I can, but until you make that decision, I can't hear your pain anymore. It hurts me to hear how terrible your life is, but there is absolutely nothing I can do to help you change it if you won't do anything to change it yourself. I'll be happy to talk about anything else any time. Let me know if you decide to make a change, and I'll do what I can to help, but until then the topic of your misery is off limits."

In effect, what my mother was saying was, "Julie, as long as you insist on being the victim, I can't help you." It was hard to hear, but I immediately understood what she meant, and it forced me to stop and look at myself. What was *I* doing? Why was I stuck here? Did I get something out of being unhappy and unwilling to change my circumstances? Why did I feel so powerless to change? The answers led me down a path that brought me closer and closer to BEing the best me I could be.

Mama's startling new position motivated me to new heights! I became proactive in trying to make positive changes in my life. Instead of just blaming and complaining, I began to read how-to books on everything from relationships to total-life transformations. By golly, I had made a mess of my life, and I was going to FIX it.

Ultimately, it didn't matter how motivated I was. As my mother requested, I kept quiet about my misery and trials while I tried everything, with the exception of God, to dig myself out of the pit I'd made. The day came when I had to make a decision to take responsibility for me and the state of my life. Though I'd like to say I made my decision after much thought and prayer, I confess that my decision was based primarily on fear. Obviously, learning how to "BE" the right kind of person was going to be a long and drawn-out process for me.

CHAPTER FOUR

HE LOVES ME,
HE LOVES ME NOT

৫৹

ABOUT THAT RELATIONSHIP WITH GOD...

People don't talk about it much, but I suspect a lot of folks have struggled as mightily and as long as I have to find God. I have certainly been through the ups and downs of sensing Him, wondering if He's gone away, wondering if He even existed in the first place, trying to force faith, doubting and then doubting again, feeling His presence, and most of all, not feeling worthy of His love.

My journey may not even come close to the one you are on, but I want to encourage those of you who are still experiencing the ups and downs, the doubt, and the feelings of an on-again/off-again relationship with God. I spent thirty-five years growing to the point of total surrender, and I'd already accepted Christ as my Savior! My first encounter with God, however, happened when I was a little kid.

THE SWAMP

I spent a lot of time outside when I was a child, climbing trees and exploring the woods and the marshy swampland across the street from our house in Columbia, South Carolina. I was captivated by the thick green moss that grew on the damp trees, the soft, fluffy ferns, and I couldn't resist checking the Venus Flytrap plants to see if they had caught their prey for the day. Big brown and little black tadpoles, water bugs, snakes, frogs, salamanders, and newts held me in rapt attention, as did the big, ugly carp that were easily caught by hand when the creek that cut through the center of our swamp ran low during the heat of summer.

A huge, smooth old log spanned the width of that creek, and I often sat right in the middle of it, staring down through the clear water to the sandy bottom below. I'd daydream and occasionally spot a turtle swimming by, a school of nervous minnows, or a sizable crawdad kicking up a cloud of sand as it backed its way into a new hiding place.

The trees that lined both banks of the creek were tall and the sunlight that shimmied its way through the dense layers of leaves danced in dapples across the glassy-smooth surface of the water. Between the birds singing, dragonflies buzzing by, and frogs calling, the swamp was a living symphony. Even the *plop, plop* of snakes dropping off tree limbs into the water was familiar enough not to be alarming. I was completely in my element, and any concern I had disappeared as soon as I ducked into the dense undergrowth that concealed my sanctuary from our neighborhood.

I was sprawled out on the old log one day, doing my usual daydreaming, when I saw something ripping through the water toward me with such speed that it left a huge V-shaped wake in its path. Heart pounding, I jumped to my feet to run away when whatever it was suddenly disappeared under the water. Insane curiosity kept me on the log, and when the creature surfaced, it was facing me no more than four feet away. My emotions raced from stark terror to amazed joy. I remember laughing out loud because my relief was so great. I was witnessing an otter in the wild.

The otter turned flips in front of me, swimming up and down the creek and from side to side, climbing onto the bank and sliding back into the water like a torpedo on a mission. He was putting on a show, and he kept looking my way to be sure I appreciated his antics. Then, as suddenly as he appeared, the otter was gone.

Laughing, I exclaimed aloud, "God, You are so funny!" I was only about nine years old, but I knew God had sent the otter and that He got a kick out of delighting me...just like any father would.

At that time in my life I had not been to church enough to know anything about God, really. I was unaware of Romans 1:20, "For the invisible things of him since the creation of the world are clearly seen, being perceived through the things that are made, even his everlasting power and divinity; that they may be without excuse" (ASV), but I had always sensed Him in His creation. I saw the plants and the animals, the wind, the rain, the sun, the mountains, the ocean, and the surf—and I knew. I knew He existed, and I knew He was GREAT and MIGHTY. I knew that He was in charge and He was in control. Somehow I knew He cared about me, and in that one special moment in the swamp I knew He had a sense of humor, and that we had shared a good laugh on me.

THE DARK SIDE

Through nature and animals I felt connected to the goodness of God. However, even as a little child, I was aware of a dark side of me that was deceptive, mean, and selfish. I felt the guilt wash over me after fibbing about what I was doing at a friend's house. I felt like the criminal I was when I stole cookies in preschool, candy off my first grade teacher's desk, and dimes off Dad's dresser to buy extra ice cream at school.

When my sister Cindy got roller skates for her eighth birthday, I cried, fussed, and complained so loudly that my parents went out and bought me a pair as well. I felt wicked every time I put those ill-gotten skates on my feet! On the way to the five-and-dime to spend our allowance, I got so jealous of my best girlfriend, Tutti Profitt, getting more money for allowance (a whole dime!) that I threw my nickel out of the car window. Then I was so envious over the little cleaning kit she bought that I dumped out the contents of her miniature Windex bottle when she wasn't looking. My little-kid heart knew I was bad and mean. I acted "ugly"—a southern term for the most unbecoming behavior possible. I felt "ugly" from the inside out, but I was at a loss for what to do about it.

My exposure to church included a couple of Vacation Bible Schools, the occasional Easter Sunday, and just enough sporadic attendance that I "went forward" when I was twelve years old and falsely professed my belief in Jesus Christ because everybody else my age had already done so. I still remember the shame and guilt I felt eating the celebratory ice cream cone we had after church the Sunday I was baptized.

On a happier note, my mother had a small, white, ceramic open-Bible piece that sat on her makeup table. The words of the Lord's Prayer were painted in gold on the two open pages. I can recall feeling reverence when I read it and a desire to memorize it word-for-word. I did memorize it, and I didn't tell anyone that I had. It was my secret, and I prayed it in my mind, over and over again.

The pull-and-tug of good versus bad was already underway. At some level I knew God existed, but I didn't give it a whole lot of thought. I was still just a kid, and the vast majority of my experiences were positive. I had loving, kind parents, and I got along well with my sister Suzan, six years my senior. I happily shared a bedroom with my next oldest sister Cindy, and when I was nine-and-a-half years old, baby brother Tom arrived, as cute as could be.

School was a bit of a rough spot because of the difficulty I had learning how to read. I was a "Yellow Bird"—"Blue Birds" were the best readers, and socially, yellow birds were not even allowed a place to roost—but the school issue disappeared as my reading improved, and I made friends easily.

When I turned eleven, my number-one birthday wish came true! My parents gave me my first horse, and all was right with the world. Smokey was jet black, and the perfect kid horse. He had been rescued off the "killer wagon" and was little more than a thirty-plus-year-old bag of bones when I got him, but it was love, love, love, at first sight! That horse was MY HORSE!

I went to bed happy and woke up happy. There were no worries or concerns in my life. Even when junior high started, I was happy. I ran for secretary-treasurer and easily won the office. My biggest concerns were when I would get to ride next, what to wear to school, and when I could get my braces off.

All of that changed when Dad suddenly announced we were moving to Texas. He had a great job opportunity, and we needed to be there in two weeks. It was scary but exciting at first. Mom and Dad explained that my horse and my sister's horse would be shipped to Dallas as soon as transportation could be found.

August 26, 1968, I celebrated my thirteenth birthday by riding the sleek and beautiful Smokey in the new riding jodhpurs and Ratcatcher shirt I got for my birthday. I'd asked to be picked up from the boarding stable as late as possible since it was the last time I'd see Smokey until he could be transported to Dallas.

When I saw the headlights of my parents' car turn into the long drive, I rushed out into the dark pasture for one last hug. Smokey's eyebrows and muzzle had long been gray, and without them I would have been hard pressed to locate him in the dark field. With tears and a promise to see him soon, I hugged my best friend good-bye.

FROM HAPPY TO HORRIFIED

We arrived in Dallas, Texas, just in time for me to start eighth grade. I became "the new girl from South Carolina" who wore long skirts and flat shoes and talked like a hick. The kids in Dallas wore makeup, miniskirts, and platform shoes, and talked about stuff I'd never heard of. I did not fit in.

Then I had the great misfortune of having a boy think I was cute, and out of jealousy, his ex-girlfriend, a popular cheerleader, started a horrible rumor about me that ruined my reputation. I was ostracized to the point that I was one of two girls in the whole grade not invited to a private party thrown by a small group of eighth-grade parents.

Suddenly I was thrust into a world I was ill-equipped to handle. I went from happy to horrified and humiliated. Then I learned that my beloved horse would not be making the trip. It had been decided that he was too old to travel the distance, and he had been given to a newly widowed man who I was told needed company.

I left behind every friend I'd ever had, I was being ridiculed and bullied, and when I learned I was losing what I loved most in the world—well, those experiences changed me forever. I wasn't naive about pain and grief and disappointment anymore. And on some level I quit caring about much of anything...most especially what happened to me. And that is when the bad choices in my life began.

First, I made a conscious decision to run with the kids who had bad reputations because I had already been lumped in with them by the vicious rumor—and they were willing to be my friend when no one reputable was. Running with them led to more bad choices that carried me further and further away from the brushes with God I'd experienced in my innocence. Ultimately, I earned the bad reputation I had been wrongly given, and I suffered the consequences of my choices for years to come.

My parents were unaware of the degree of my suffering and had no idea I was living a life they couldn't have even imagined. When I was at home I was compliant, easygoing, and responsible. By then I had learned how to make good grades, and I was holding down a part-time job. There were no outward signs that anything was wrong. I was never late for my curfew; I never spoke disrespectfully to my parents or to any authority figure; and I readily did as I was asked. I was choosing to keep my problems to myself, and I knew how to put on a happy face. Regrettably, each bad choice led to another bad choice, and soon my life was truly cascading out of control.

My high school English teacher, Mrs. Gwaltney, noticed that I couldn't stay awake in class and talked with me one day to find out what was going on. I love her to this day for trying, but I told her I had to work late most nights, and I did work late—but not because I had to. The truth was I kept myself busy every second of the day and night until I crashed into bed too exhausted to think. Between school, work, the tennis team, my new horse, and dating, I never rested. To be still meant time to contemplate my predicament.

Some months before Dad accepted Jesus Christ as his Lord and Savior on July 4, 1972, he sent my two sisters and me to a Bill Gothard Basic Youth Conflicts Seminar. I was sixteen years old. I've been asked why he did that if he wasn't a Christian, and the answer is that Dad had heard it was a good seminar for young people, and my father was one of those people who thought he believed in Jesus because his mother had taken him to church every time the doors opened. He didn't understand that his mother was the one with the relationship, not him! Also, Dad had a history of sending us to seminars he thought might help us be better, stronger, smarter, or more enthusiastic people. He believed in seminars! Unfortunately, he couldn't attend them with us because of the amount of traveling he did, so we went without him.

By the second day of the Basic Youth Conflicts Seminar, my sisters refused to go, but I was drawn back to the event. I arrived alone, not sure what to expect, but I left with Jesus in my heart. Somehow, I felt shy about telling anyone what I had experienced. It was almost too sacred to share, and I wasn't sure it had really happened. That night I became sure.

On the floor of my bedroom I confessed all of my sins, I repented and wept, and when I was completely spent I literally, physically, felt the comforting caress of God's hands on my shoulders. I knew that I had Jesus in my heart, and my joy knew no bounds!

I had high hopes for the new and changed life I was going to lead. I was praying constantly, but I didn't tell anyone about my conversion. Within three weeks, being unchurched and undiscipled, I fell back into my old pattern and committed a sin I had promised God I'd never do again. I was filled with gut-wrenching remorse, and I did not understand grace. I believed that I had blown my only chance to have a relationship with Jesus, so I proceeded to live outside of God's will for almost two more decades, burying my soul in secrets and shame.

CHAPTER FIVE

DIFFERENT CHOICES

THE KING OF GOOD CHOICES

I like to say my father is the king of good choices, and what I mean by that is it seems as though Dad was born with the innate ability to immediately know when something is bad for him. My grandmother also helped influence the quality of his "choice picker" by teaching all of her children right from wrong. She took every life opportunity to point out good choices and bad ones.

One day Dad's mother commented that a particular man who was respected for his business success and his volunteerism in the community was the "worst possible kind of drinker."

Dad asked, "What do you mean, Mama? That man is successful, he has a good family, and he goes to church every Sunday. It doesn't look to me like he has a drinking problem." My grandmother explained that my dad's impression of the man was the very reason his drinking was such a problem. She said that he was setting an example that a few drinks every evening were okay, and maybe even part of the trappings of success. The problem was that others who admired his success and position in the community might want to emulate him and start drinking every evening, only to discover that they couldn't control their alcohol consumption like Mr. Success, and they would lose all that they loved and valued.

My grandmother was speaking from experience. Two of her older children had married alcoholics and suffered because of their spouses' addictions. She was doing everything she could to educate the children who were still under her roof not to get involved in something that might hurt them or the ones they loved.

I know that my grandmother's early teaching and knowledge of how his siblings were hurt by alcoholism influenced Dad's thinking. He shared with me that the first time he had too much to drink he realized that he REALLY liked the way it made him feel—so he determined never to do that again!

The same thing happened when he tried his hand at a little gambling when he was in college. Shooting dice for double-or-nothing when he was selling sandwiches really got his adrenaline going, but one night he lost every dime and sandwich and had to borrow money for a taxi ride home. He instinctively, and with the help of consequences, knew gambling was something he could get into trouble with, so he simply refused to ever do it again. Dad's practical application of that wisdom proved to be a huge blessing in his life. I consider it nothing short of a miracle that Dad didn't let his compulsive personality get the best of him.

Another area of good choices in which my father has excelled is marriage. My dad has been the example of marital happiness for many through the years by sharing how he has protected his most important relationship on earth, the relationship he has with my mother. We knew from the time we were little that Dad's relationship with Mom took priority. When Dad got back in town he'd always take Mom out to dinner so they could catch up and have time alone. Somehow, knowing our parents were true partners gave us security that nothing else could have.

Dad also made the conscious good choice to honor his wife by not allowing his children to speak to his beloved with a tone of disrespect. He made it clear that our mother held the primary position as his mate and life partner and that while he loved us deeply, he loved her first and foremost. If we treated his beloved with anything other than the utmost respect, we were "skating on thin ice," as Dad is apt to say.

Another lifelong rule Dad has held is that he never goes anywhere alone with a woman who is not his wife or daughter. Not to lunch or dinner or even in a car. He never closed his office door if a female was visiting with him. In the thirty-four years my Dad has worked with his executive assistant, Laurie Magers, he has never been alone with her. Dad understands that temptation strikes when you least expect it, and he determined not to put himself or anyone else in a vulnerable position. He also knows how rumors get started, and he wasn't about to give anyone even the slightest reason to talk. Tongues wag about what looks bad as if it is bad, so we mustn't even give the impression of wrongdoing. That choice has served him well.

My grandmother wasn't the only one who influenced my father. Through the years I've heard many stories from my father about people, from teachers to former bosses, who cared enough to share their advice and take a special interest in helping him make wise choices. And I'm so glad he chose to listen—in my eyes, Dad truly is the King of Good Choices.

THE POSTER CHILD FOR BAD CHOICES

I, on the other hand, seem to be a natural as the poster child for bad choices. By his own admission, I got Dad's compulsive personality—except in my case it came without the auto-stop Dad seemed to possess. I never could get enough of the stuff I loved, and I seemed to love just about everything! Between the two of us, Dad and I can cover every topic imaginable from personal experience. He can tell you the benefits of what will happen when you make the right choice, and I can tell you the consequences of making the wrong choice.

When I was a little girl, my family used to quietly take verbal bets on which dessert I would pick when we got to the end of the cafeteria line. As soon as I picked up the prettiest, most colorful dessert offered, they'd all congratulate themselves for knowing me so well. I'm sorry to say that I was every bit as predictable when it came to good-versus-bad choices. It was a given that I'd make the worst choice possible, and that was because I was making choices not just for myself, but for what I thought somebody else wanted me to do. I didn't want to let anyone down, and ultimately I let everyone down, especially myself.

Unlike Dad, I had not been told of any possible consequence of drinking alcohol, with the exception of Dad telling me I shouldn't try to get into clubs or bars while I was underage because the proprietor could lose his/her liquor license as a result of my deception. It was a given that underage drinking was illegal, and I was expected not to break any laws. Dad often shared practical cause-and-effect consequences with me. He did the best he could without the benefit of the Instruction Manual.

My grandmother based her instruction to my father about not setting an example that might bring harm to others on Romans 14:21: "It is good neither to eat flesh, nor to drink wine, nor any thing whereby thy brother stumbleth, or is offended, or is made weak" (KJV).

While the Scripture makes it clear that Christians have freedom in Christ to drink and eat anything, God's Word also tells us not to be gluttonous or to drink to excess—two forms of disobedience that lead to harsh and even fatal consequences on occasion.

I was weak and full of stumbles. It was October 1969, and I was fourteen years old the first time I drank, which also marks my first black-out drunk. Until the moment I passed out, I felt like I had arrived.

I had gotten permission to go with my boyfriend and a big group to an outdoor concert. Woodstock, the music festival of all music festivals, had taken place a few months before, and outdoor concerts were all the rage. I'm not sure how my boy-friend got me inside my house without my mother realizing I was drunk, but Dad was out of town, and I didn't get caught. I'll never understand why my boyfriend didn't break up with me after that embarrassing event, but he didn't.

The first time I took a drag on a cigarette I was also fourteen, and I felt like I had come home! I never coughed or gagged or even sputtered. I smoked a whole pack the first night and ulti-mately became a three-plus-pack-per-day smoker.

I truly was a natural at immediate, full-blown addiction! If a little bit was good, a whole lot was way, way better!

I approached desserts and bread the same way, and my love affair with refined sugar and simple carbohydrates made me a liar and a thief at as early as four years of age. It escalated to yo-yo dieting and culminated with a revelation that I had made sweets and simple carbohydrates a god in my life, to be sought after at all hours of the day and night.

Even things that are normally considered good can be destruc-tive when we get compulsive about them. That was the case with my reading! I didn't read a book the first three years I was married to my second husband because I didn't want him to know that everything came to a dead stop when I got involved with a good book. I'd delay cooking, cleaning, carpool, sleeping—you name it, so that I could finish my book. The chaos my book reading caused for a family of six was not pleasant, and the repercussions generally involved a lot of apologizing: "Sorry I'm late," "Sorry I burned the roast," "Sorry I overslept," "Sorry I didn't remember your practice," etc.

CHOICES DO HAVE CONSEQUENCES

I still cringe when I recall the look of confusion on my mother's face. I could see her furrowed brow through the beveled glass panes of the front door as she hurriedly pulled on her bathrobe and rushed to answer the incessant ringing of the doorbell. I was hiding, as best I could, behind the police officer who had given me a ride home at six o'clock that morning. The officer explained he had discovered me riding around in a car with some boys he knew to be "trouble." The jig was up. I'd been caught sneaking out.

I was fifteen years old, and I had been forbidden to see a boy I liked...who happened to be eighteen. I wasn't allowed to single date, but I had asked if the boy could come visit me at our home. When the request was denied, I was told not only was he not welcome in our home, but I was never to speak with him again. (Amazing how this makes perfect sense to me now.)

I was heartbroken and didn't understand the reasoning, so my forbidden boyfriend often called me on my father's office phone at the far end of the house after everyone was in bed for the night. (Secretive phone calls were harder to achieve before cell phones came into being.) One night he said he was calling from a payphone nearby and suggested I crawl out of the window and go for a short ride with him. Without considering the consequences, I did just that.

I don't know how many times I snuck out before I was brought home by the police officer, but I never did it again!

Nobody in our family had ever snuck out at night. Neither of my sisters wanted to spend as much time away from home as I did. They never had a desire to work while they were still in school, and they seemed content to come home and watch TV or talk on the phone. We didn't hang out together and I think it is just as well. I would have been a bad influence on Cindy for sure. My behavior, by comparison, was truly scandalous. Our family was so unfamiliar with bad behavior that there had never even been a discussion about not sneaking out.

I was asked what I thought my punishment should be, so I socked it to me. I said, "Ground me for a month! No phone, no friends, no after-school activities." I knew I deserved it, and I was relieved to get to pay my dues, and if you can fathom this, I was relieved to have an excuse to say no. I felt so obligated to do anything I was asked to do, I was glad to be able to say I had gotten caught and that I was unwilling to chance the punishment again.

Two weeks into my "grounding," I came down with a dangerously bad case of mononucleosis (thanks to my home economics kitchen lab partner) that was accompanied by strep throat and a fever that caused hallucinations. One night I thought there were two neighborhood boys (who were brothers) in my room asking me to sneak out and I kept telling them no, go away, that I didn't want any more trouble.

A few days after my fever broke, my father came to my room to ask about muddy footprints they had discovered leading from the window to my bedside. Until that moment I did not know the boys had been real!

Dad asked for names and I gave them. He visited the young men's home, spoke to their father, and if I am remembering correctly, had a police officer explain what the consequences were for breaking and entering and what might have happened to them in a home where intruders are met with a gun.

Unfortunately, the boys were so angry that I had divulged their names and gotten them in trouble, they began calling me vulgar names in the school hallways and yelling lewd things across the parking lot or on the tennis courts where we all practiced. The consequences of my choices were starting to have a domino effect. I had done no wrong in regard to those two boys, but my reputation was already in place and their antics just accentuated and aggravated the misery I lived with.

The problem I had with the brothers compelled me to speak with a school counselor about early graduation. She agreed that I needed to get off our campus and helped me plan a schedule that allowed me to get the last hour of credit I needed from night school and still graduate with my class. I didn't attend a single day of senior classes at my high school, and while that choice made me very happy, it also resulted in my life jumping ahead of where it should have been.

The year most kids spend excited about homecoming, dances, senior trips, and senior proms, I was working a full-time job and going twice a week to night school. I loved working and making my own money, but my choice elevated my dating to an "older" crowd, and I found myself engaged to a twenty-six-year-old man when I was only seventeen. I just couldn't grow up fast enough, and yes, you guessed it, my parents were not pleased with that development, but they didn't have to be concerned very long. I broke the engagement after about three months, and in true Bad Choice Julie fashion, it didn't take long for me to jump out of the frying pan and into the fire!

My father's good choices had positive consequences—a pristine, flawless, reputation for integrity and freedom from habits that destroy; my bad choices had negative consequences that seemed to never end.

CHAPTER SIX

THE REAL ISSUES OF CHOICE MAKING

TWO LEVELS OF CHOICE MAKING

We make choices based on what we want and are afraid we can't get, or we make choices based on faith and the power of God we have within.

Being a creature of free will, I have long been in the habit of exercising my God-given ability to make choices. I also happen to have a sin nature that creates a constant, natural drive to do evil. Understanding those basic facts makes it pretty easy to understand why I was naturally drawn to make choices that are not what God would want for me and that led to no good.

God's desire for me has always been that I surrender my life to Him to the extent that my choices are based on His will and not mine. Until I did that, I was actually incapable of making the best possible choices or being the right kind of person. Without faith and God's power, I was rudderless.

As a new, unchurched Christian, I was unaware of what God had to say about my sin, my salvation, His grace, His will, and the way I was to live out my life as a believer in Jesus Christ. I didn't have a clue about what was in the Bible and didn't go anywhere for help with my question: "I'm saved, now what?"

There are some people who would argue that I was not truly saved at that Bill Gothard seminar. They'd say that I would have been incapable of sinning (deliberately breaking God's moral law) the way I did after my salvation experience, had it been genuine. But here is the sincere truth: that experience, whatever you choose to call it, completely screwed up my sinning. I never sinned again without great guilt, shame, remorse, and bitter regret because I had "knowledge" of what sin was. Unfortunately, I didn't have the knowledge of God's grace.

My inability to understand that God's grace covered future sins as well as past ones set me up for the struggle of my life. When I accepted Jesus and repented, I sincerely thought that I would never sin again; when I did sin, I was mortified. I felt such an all-consuming love for Jesus I couldn't believe that I had done what I did not want to do. My shame drove my self-esteem to a new all-time low. I had experienced the love of my Lord, and was suddenly aware of the extreme difference between living in the darkness of my self-will and living in the light of God's love. The contrast was vast, and I felt hopeless and beyond redemption.

Each time I sinned, I felt like I had broken the heart of God again! I believed I'd blown my only chance at a happy life. If only I had read all the stories that God, in His great wisdom, included in the Bible—stories of men and women who loved Him, yet still sinned. If only I had known that God's love and forgiveness were not based upon my performance. In my mind, once I had sinned, there was nothing left to lose, so I continued on in a godless fashion.

INTO THE FIRE

In the fall of 1973, I was eighteen years old, living with my parents and taking classes at a local junior college. For the first time in four years, I was not working, or engaged, or going steady with anyone. I was enjoying my school work and riding and showing my horse. The need to study kept me out of my usual trouble, and fortunately my reputation hadn't followed me to college. There was a breather of sorts, and I was as content as I could remember being since we'd moved to Texas.

All of that changed one weekend in November. I was showing my Thoroughbred gelding, Butter Rum, at a three-day event in McKinney, Texas, when I met my first real cowboy, a horse trader named Jim. Jim was the spitting image of the "Marlboro Man" in his cowboy hat, western boots, and championship belt buckle. He was tall and fit, and he had sparkling blue eyes and a mischievous grin—all of which got my attention, but the biggest attraction was that he actually knew how to ride a horse. Here was a man I had something in common with, and he was asking for my help showing his horses.

Our first date was November 15. I remember it because it happened to be his birthday—his thirtieth birthday, he said. I was a little put off by the age difference, but I rationalized it by asking myself how much different could thirty be when compared to my twenty-six-year-old ex-fiancé. In my mind the answer came back in simple math: four years! Four years can't be bad. I never thought about Jim being twelve years older than me.

Eight months later we went to get our marriage license. I was shocked to discover that Jim was actually thirty-six years old, not thirty, as he had told me. He asked me to forgive him because he was sure I would not have dated him if I had known he was thirty-six. He seemed sincere in his apology and he was right, I would not have dated him! I rationalized this discrepancy away by deciding I loved him when I thought he was thirty, so why would six years change how I felt about him?

My parents did what they could to convince me that eighteen years was too big of an age difference. Dad and Mom seriously tried to stop the wedding (Jim and I had planned it overnight and sprung it on them the next morning), but they had a flat tire and then got lost. Dad even called the pastor and implored him not to perform the ceremony. I was at that know-it-all stage, and though I had serious doubts for other reasons, I couldn't deny an intense attraction to him. Ultimately, I married him to make myself feel better. I had secretly been living with Jim and I believed the only way I could make things right in God's eyes was to marry him.

Our wedding night brought relief that I wasn't sinning sexually anymore, but our problems were just beginning. The next morning my new husband gave me a list with the names of several different banks, their addresses, and the amount of the hot checks he had written and told me to go pick them up. Even at eighteen I didn't think we were off to a very good start.

After we married, without my knowledge, my father hired a private investigator to sort out the facts about my husband. When Dad got the report, he called to say my husband had several failed marriages in his past and at least four children with three different women. I also learned his "best friend," who visited every so often, was actually his parole officer. The good news was that Jim didn't have a history of violent criminal acts; he just had a problem with hot checks, forgery, unpaid hotel rooms, and five alias names. Trust was fast becoming an issue.

Dad told me I could get an annulment based on the fact that Jim had lied about his past, but I wanted to honor the marriage commitment and honestly believed that I could make it work. To my parents' credit, when they realized I was going to stay in the marriage, they did what they could to make Jim feel welcome in the family.

The first few times my husband told me how things were going to be I thought he was teasing. He said, "Woman, you make the tea, I'll drink it. You cook the food, I'll eat it. You clean the house, I'll mess it up. You feed the dog, I'll pet it. You make the bed, I'll sleep in it. You wash the clothes, I'll wear them." He told me he expected dinner to be hot on the table when he walked in, and he expected his slacks and shirts to be wrinkle-free. If they weren't, I heard about it loud and clear.

I went from enjoying doing things for him to trembling when I'd hear his truck coming up the driveway. If I didn't have everything done the way he wanted it done, he'd get furious with me. I'd never been yelled at in my life, and I cowed under his angry, harsh words.

I had hoped that things would level out after our daughter was born, but my husband struggled with the division of my attention.

My father had taught me that there were only two reasons I could ever come home after I got married. One was if my husband became a "habitual" adulterer and the other was if my husband ever hit me. Three years, eleven moves, and one three-month-old baby later I went home.

My husband had so much experience with divorce that he knew how to keep it simple. The day after I left him with only the clothes on my back and our baby girl, he sold everything in our rented house to one man—including our daughter's clothes and crib.

My choice to ignore my parents' warnings culminated in me being a twenty-one-year-old single mother without a college education. My daughter was the saving grace, the gift and the blessing of my marriage. There was no other reason I could come up with for the hardship of the years I lived with my husband. I just knew Amey was supposed to be here and she was supposed to be mine.

My parents allowed me to live with them for the next eighteen months. I had to get a job, buy a car, save up money for an apartment, and start from scratch. It took about five months for the divorce to be final, and when it was over I was devastated by all that had happened and sickened that I was divorced. I had expected relief, not grief, on the day our divorce was final. The truth is divorce stinks, even when you think you need one... and God hates divorce.

WAIT! I MADE ONE GOOD CHOICE!

Of all the different topics my father has taught over the years, I am especially grateful to have understood and believed one of his philosophies early on. I heard Dad say many times over the years that children see themselves as an extension of their parents. If the child believes his parent is a bad person, the child will believe he/she, too, is a bad person.

I determined that I would never say cutting, hurtful, degrading remarks about my daughter's father to her. Our divorce happened for reasons that she had no part in, and I was not going to get her involved in grown-up stuff that should not concern her. I decided if she ever asked me a point-blank question (and she eventually did), I would answer her honestly, but I would not elaborate.

I knew when we divorced that my husband would not pay child support regularly, if at all. I accepted that as a fact and made it my mission to be sure he supported our daughter emotionally by spending time with her on a regular basis, even if he couldn't/ wouldn't support her financially.

The money would have been helpful, but of far more importance was my daughter knowing—really knowing— her father. When divorce does happen, it should be every parent's goal to set aside their differences and do what is best for their children. Nothing is harder than watching innocent children torn to pieces as their parents pull them this way and that, trying to make them pick which "side" they are on. It is alarming how often this scenario plays out in homes across the world! When I see that tug-of-war going on, I want to say, "Hello!!! Who are the children here? GROW UP! GET A LIFE!"

My ex-husband and I forgave each other early on and have a friendly relationship to this day. We did work together to do what was best for our daughter, and visitation was what we determined worked best for us. If Jim couldn't have Amey on his court-appointed weekend, we just agreed that he'd get her the next time he could, regardless of whether it was a court-appointed weekend or not. After he moved out of town, he came to see her every time he was back working in our area.

In fact, I only got tough with Jim about visitation when he wasn't coming around enough. Over the years there was an ebb and flow to his involvement with our daughter, and I'm happy to say that he is now seeing her and the four beautiful grandchildren she has blessed us with on a very regular basis. The little ones love their Cowboy Granddad, and I am so glad they do!

Thank You, Jesus, for making this happy ending out of our early mistakes, and thank you, Daddy, for teaching me that tearing others down, for any reason, tears everyone down.

(In case you're wondering, I had my daughter read what you've just read to be sure she was okay with it. I learned that from my father too. He always asked us to read and approve anything he wrote about us in any of his books. Smart man, that daddy of mine!)

CHAPTER SEVEN

THE SINGLE-PARENT YEARS

※

PLEASE STAY

I meet people all the time who assume because my father has done well in life and in business that I, too, enjoy his financial blessings. WRONG! I'm not complaining—just setting the facts straight. I was a single parent like any other single parent. We had a deal in our family: At age eighteen, we were either in college, married, or out working to support ourselves. In our family, that was the normal progression of life.

At eighteen, I was in college, and when I married a few months shy of my nineteenth birthday, I was under the financial umbrella of my husband. When we separated, I only had one option, and that was my parents' home. I've always been grateful that my parents gave me that leg-up when I needed it so badly.

I tried to be as unobtrusive as possible. My brother was only eleven years old when my daughter and I moved back in. Mom, Dad, and Tom had established a living routine of their own in the three years I had been away, and I didn't want to inconvenience anyone.

Little Amey and I took the guest room that was at the opposite end of the house from the rest of the bedrooms. That way if Amey cried at night nobody would lose any sleep. I did what I could to help, including my share of the cooking and dishes, and I started working as soon as I could.

Everything went well until Amey's eighteen-month check-up when her pediatrician asked me if she was sleeping in a separate room yet. When I said no, he explained that the longer I put off getting her into her own room, the more resentful and displaced she would feel if I ever remarried. He made it very clear that Amey's mental health and my future marriage would be in jeopardy if I didn't take care of that issue, and he said the sooner the better!

I went home and told my parents it was time for me to get my own place, and not just because Amey needed her own room. I also believed it was time for me to cut the apron strings, and I was comfortable that I had enough money saved in case of an emergency. Dad seriously tried to get me to stay, which made me feel good, but I needed to do what was best for my daughter. It took me a few months to get everything organized, but the day came that I was on my own for the first time in my life.

THE TREADMILL

I quickly learned how tightly I had to manage our budget. I was proud to be making it happen, but it brought a level of stress I'd never experienced in the past. Being the only one to provide food, shelter, and clothing for a child was a big responsibility, and though I'd had a good bit of work experience before I married, it wasn't the kind of work that brought in big money.

My night job waiting tables at Old San Francisco Steakhouse, an upscale restaurant in Dallas, Texas, provided more income than an office job, and it allowed me to be with my daughter during most of her waking hours. Having an infant made that condition of employment far more important to me than money. I was even willing to wear the company-issued replica of a nineteenth-century dance hall costume: a black can-can style dress trimmed with red ruffles, fishnet stockings that bit into my toes, a garter belt, and high heels! Fortunately, the costume wasn't overly revealing, but I did have a lot of explaining to do the night I got pulled over for accidentally exceeding the speed limit on my way home!

When Amey was a toddler, I added more income by taking a job as a weekend leasing agent at an apartment complex. That position eventually led me to quit the restaurant to manage the 220-unit property.

The only place I truly excelled was in my work. I had an incredibly strong work ethic (thank you, Daddy), and I wasn't afraid of hard work. So, while our income improved and our standard of living went up, the pressure to continue to succeed increased. I was finally getting some positive feedback from at least one of my behaviors, but the stress led to alcohol use, which led to more bad choices—especially in relationships.

I had no idea that being on my own would make me so vulnerable. I had not dated much when I lived with my folks. I wasn't ready, and it was awkward being picked up at my parents' house. I didn't realize how good I'd had it and how much safer that situation was than the one I faced when men came to my house to pick me up for a date. I had a few scares, but mostly I discovered that I was extremely wary about men, and for some sick reason I still felt obligated to do as they pleased, even when it didn't please me. That led to bad choices in short-term relationships, and it contributed to even more excessive alcohol consumption to offset my mounting feelings of zero self-worth.

Bad choices became a habit in my life. One led to another, and as I felt worse and worse about the choices I was making, I began to lose hope that I would ever be able to change. But I kept trying.

Over the next five-plus years I changed jobs four times, and each job was a step up the ladder to success. The steps up that ladder took more and more time away from my little girl, but I didn't know how to get off the treadmill or even understand fully all that was motivating me to work longer and longer hours. I was so proud to be able to buy my own house after starting from nothing six years earlier, and with the exception of my mortgage, I was debt free. I was finally enjoying the kind of financial security I had always dreamed of, but at what price?

SEEKING GOD

Since the day I left my husband, I began seeking the relationship with God that I believed I had lost shortly after I came to know Him. I went to a single parents' Sunday school class and to church every week. Amey and I attended single-parent functions and group activities, and I tried to study my Bible. Unfortunately, alcohol and sexual sin kept getting in the way. My guilt, my shame, and my regret at doing that which I did not want to do kept me from feeling worthy of a relationship with Jesus.

I kept going to church because I knew the answer was with Him. I knew it in the depths of my soul, but I couldn't figure out how to get good enough to be His. So, I'd sin and go to church. I knew I was in the right place, even if I didn't feel worthy to be there.

At one point I had a relationship with a man I thought I was going to marry. When he broke up with me, I went into a depression that was beyond anything I had ever experienced. I called my dad and asked, "Daddy, what do you do when you've read all the self-help books and you don't know what else to do? I'm so depressed I can't even move." Daddy said, "It sounds to me like you need to be spending a lot more time with your father!" I knew what he meant. He asked me if I wanted to go on his next trip out of town, but my heart heard the real truth in what Dad said. I needed to be spending a lot more time with my heavenly Father.

My progress toward a relationship with Christ was slow, slow, slow, but even as I was suffering the consequences of my bad choices, I was beginning to learn about the character of God and to understand His promises. I was growing a stronger desire to know Him, and with that desire I began to consider God's influence in my life.

A REVISED PLAN

For several years the majority of my first dates were also my last dates. When you are a single mother, any time spent on a date is time not spent with your child. My dates had to count! I'd go out with someone and if I thought there was any reason—any teeny tiny reason—they wouldn't be the right spouse for me, that was it. Those first few years, anything that reminded me in the least of my ex-husband was an immediate show stopper. The longer I was single, the more particular I got.

Finally, on January 1, 1983, I threw out the list! I threw out the legal sheet–length list I had compiled stating the qualities and qualifications for my future husband. The list included height, weight, waist size, inseam, hair color, eye color, income bracket, career, age range, church affiliation—it was thoroughly thought out. I even had a nobody-over-ten-years-older-than-me rule, for obvious reasons. I surrendered the particulars to God with a prayer that went something like this: "God, You know I've been telling You exactly what I want in a husband and how I wanted

You to arrange everything, and that hasn't been working out very well. So, if it is in Your plan that I am never to remarry, would You please remove the desire for a husband from my heart and make me content? For now, I'll just date anyone who seems nice and who believes in You, and I'll forget about all of my qualifications. I trust that You know better than I do who, if anyone, is right for me."

After I threw out the list, my cousin Sara Kathleen reassured me that "He whose name is Love will send the best!" I desperately wanted that to be the case, but I was comforting myself with the knowledge that the apostle Paul never married and he seemed to be satisfied with the fact that there was more time to spend with God if he stayed single.

Three months later I had my first date with my second husband.

I'd known him for several years—in fact, the last two companies I had worked for had specifically asked me to call on him because he was a tough customer. They thought a woman might have a better chance at getting in the door to sell him our products. His reputation for being hard on salespeople was intimidating, but we had mutual friends, so I asked for a formal introduction and that helped break the ice. I got in the door, but I never sold him a thing!

The first time I went out with Jim Norman I knew I had met the man for me. (And yes, I do have a track record for marrying men named Jim, but the similarities between the men stop there!) Our mutual friends who dined with us that night thought we must have been dating for quite some time because of how well we got along, but March 23, 1983, was our first date.

We were smitten with one another, and the relationship progressed rapidly in spite of the fifty miles between Jim's front door and mine. Our first full month of long-distance calls ran over eight hundred dollars. That's when Jim presented his less-than-bright idea. He said, "It's obvious this relationship is getting pretty serious and I've been thinking it would be a good idea for us to be able to spend more time together in person. I think you ought to let me help you get a job over here in Ft. Worth. I don't really like how many hours you have to work, and I think you make business calls in dangerous areas. You can sell your house and rent one of the townhomes in my parents' complex, and they can watch the kids for us while we go out. That way we can find out if this relationship is really going anywhere."

LONG PAUSE.

I replied, "So, what you are saying is you think I should give up everything I've worked for these past seven years, pack up and move to a new area where I don't have friends or family, and start a new job on the off chance that you might decide to marry me? If that's what you're saying...if you think I'm geographically undesirable and it's not worth the fifty-mile drive, then we don't need to be dating. I need to go to bed, and you need to think about what I said. I'm not moving."

The next afternoon Jim surprised me with the most beautiful engagement ring I'd ever seen! Six weeks later, with Dad's blessing (I had learned the hard way that first time), on June 25,

1983, we were married. I had met the perfect match for me. We had more in common than either one of us realized—which is, I'm sorry to say, not always a particularly good thing.

Too Much Blending

We combined our households and began the process of "blending" our family. My daughter Amey was six weeks shy of being seven years old, and Jim's twins from his first marriage, Little Jim and Jenni, had just turned twelve. Jim's oldest daughter, whom Jim step-parented from the age of six and adopted when she turned eighteen, was in college, but asked if she could move home as soon as the semester was over.

DeDe was nineteen, but she told me she had never had a family that sat down at the dinner table to eat together every night, and she couldn't wait to be a part of that. I was especially touched by her eagerness to join us, because I was only eight and a half years older than she. Our relationship to this day remains one of mother-daughter closeness.

Unfortunately, children weren't the only thing we were blending. It seems a great deal of our immediate attraction was based on the fact that we both enjoyed our drinks and didn't limit one another with judgmental frowns of disapproval when we'd order the second, third, fourth, or even fifth round. Nobody was counting, and I'd never experienced that before. I'd always felt limited in how much I could drink, either by my date who made it clear he wasn't going to spring for more than one or two, or by my single-parent budget. Money was no longer a deterrent.

While we were dating, I heard that Jim's ex-wife had accused him of being an alcoholic in their divorce proceedings. I'm pretty sure we'd both had several drinks before I got up the courage to ask him about the rumor. Jim said he would consider himself a heavy drinker "at times," but he didn't think he was an alcoholic.

Yes, I had married a successful, high-functioning alcoholic who enjoyed his drinks as much as I did. Sadly, it didn't take long to discover that my husband had been doing "controlled drinking" while we were dating.

Three months into our blissful marriage, Jim was passing out every night by eight or nine o'clock, and I was on my own taking care of our family. I'm not sure if I was madder about him leaving everything up to me or if I was more upset that I didn't get to be as irresponsible as he was. I just knew I was UNHAPPY.

By then I was having adjustment problems with our middle daughter, Jenni, and she and Amey were having problems getting along. All was not well in Normanville.

CHAPTER EIGHT

PROGRESS, NOT PERFECTION

❧

GOD'S INSTRUMENTS

Right from the get-go—even through our alcoholic haze— Jim and I knew that a big part of the attraction we had to one another was our desire for a Christian life. We were actively seeking a closer walk with God and headed in that direction the best way we knew how. God kept sending His people to help us find our way back to Him. We didn't always recognize His helping hand in the moment, but when we did, we were amazed!

God's first instrument was the family doctor I chose for us because of a refrigerator magnet (discerning woman that I am) included in the "Welcome Basket" we received when we moved into our new home. I had seen the doctor several times with the children and on my own before Jim finally met him. It was after

Jim's initial visit that the doctor asked me if we could speak privately. His words shook my world. "When you get sick and tired of living with a drunk, you give me a call. I have the number of a man who can get you the help you need."

At the time I was still in denial that there was any real problem. I asked why the doctor thought there was a problem, and he replied that there was no mistaking the bloodshot, yellow eyes of a serious drunk. His statement forever changed the way I saw my husband. His eyes were yellow, and they were bloodshot. I made a note to myself to remember the doctor's offer.

God's Plumber

Sure enough, my husband's drinking escalated, and I was getting increasingly vocal about my unhappiness with the problems caused by his drinking. One day in March of 1986, our kitchen sink stopped up, and about an hour before the plumber was scheduled to arrive, my husband and I began to have one of those seriously uncomfortable husband/wife discussions. The subject, once again, was Jim's drinking. I told him I loved him, but couldn't stand watching him slowly kill himself. I told him I'd keep the kids so he could get an apartment and figure out what he wanted to do about his drinking problem.

Just as our discussion was reaching its most heated level, the plumber arrived. Jim was visibly upset and agitated—and, he told me later, feeling scared to death. I was wiping tears off my cheeks and feeling hopeless and emotionally exhausted. The unsuspecting plumber entered this scene with a disgustingly cheerful attitude, dragging his Roto-Rooter behind him.

That plumber smiled the entire time he attacked the sink with his Roto-Rooter, and even tried to joke with us. Our emotional sparks were a stark contrast to his happy attitude. When the sink drain was cleared, Mr. Plumber sat down at the kitchen table with us to make out his bill. He was talking away about his kids when he suddenly paused and said, "You know...I'm an alcoholic!"

If Jim could have brought the fires of hell upon that man he would have done it right then! I could not believe what I had just heard. And did he stop there? Oh no, the man went on and on about all the problems alcohol had caused during his life. He talked about wrecked vehicles and wrecked relationships. He talked about financial disasters and time spent in jails for public intoxication. He talked about hangovers and headaches. He talked and talked and talked. The more he talked, the closer he came to having Jim strangle him with the cable of his Roto-Rooter.

Then, the plumber looked right at Jim and smiled. He said he had not taken a drink in a long time and all of those bad things were behind him. He said he belonged to an anonymous fellowship of former drinkers and had learned to live happily without alcohol. Then, he handed Jim the bill and stopped talking.

Jim paid the man, and he left. I felt as if the heavens had opened up and the "Hallelujah Chorus" was filling the room. Neither of us dared to speak a word about what had just transpired. You would have thought we had received the visitation of an angel. All I know is that today we refer to that man as God's plumber!

The brush with God's plumber did not cause Jim to stop drinking, but it did prepare him for the next turn of events.

HONEY, I'M TURNING YOU OVER TO GOD!

Just as the doctor had predicted, the day arrived when I was sick and tired of being married to a drunk. It happened on the heels of the worst drinking binge I'd ever seen my husband have. On April 5, 1986, Jim and I went to dinner with friends at a Chinese restaurant. Jim drank a few bottles of hot saki, mai tais, Scotch and water, cognac, etc. By the time we got home he was obviously feeling a buzz, but he kept drinking until the only thing left in the house was a sweet liqueur that he detested. He was just finishing off the bottle of liqueur when he passed out right in front of our friends! I was embarrassed, disgusted, and humiliated. After I walked our friends out to their car, I did something I'd never done. I left Jim fully clothed and passed out in the chair and went to bed.

I was finally sick and tired of living with a drunk, so the next morning I called my doctor to get the number of the man he said could help me.

My conversation with that man was not what I expected. When he answered his phone, I told him that his friend, my doctor, had said he could help me, that I was married to a drunk and needed to know what to do about it. I got an earful!

"First," he said, "you need to understand that a normal woman wouldn't choose to marry a drunk. Let's start right there. A normal woman would leave a drunk in the dust and get on with her life. You get something out of this, or you wouldn't have married him in the first place. There isn't anything you can do about him or for him, so the only thing left to do is for you to get better. Even if you leave him, you'll go out and find yourself another drunk. Leaving him isn't the answer."

Then he asked me if I understood that I was as sick as my husband and that I needed help. I was in shock, but I did get what he was saying, so I agreed with him. He told me to get in the phone book and locate a twelve-step meeting for friends and family members of alcoholics and go that very night. He asked me to call him the next day and tell him where I went and what I learned.

The next evening, Jim, as he occasionally did after a particularly bad night, decided not to drink. He was lying on the bed reading a book on spiritual surrender when I went to tell him I was going to a meeting that helps friends and family members of alcoholics. He had no trouble concluding that he was the alcoholic in question.

Jim was still lying in bed reading his book when I got home from the meeting. I sat down on the edge of the bed and announced that I had turned him over to God and I was going to start focusing on making myself healthier because there wasn't anything I could do about him. (It's amazing what you can learn in one hour.) Jim was speechless.

I called my doctor's friend the next day to report that I had gone to a meeting and that I had turned my husband over to the care of God and I was going to be doing what it took for me to get better. With that, the gentleman told me to keep going to meetings and that there wasn't any more he could do for me. We never spoke again. It blew me away that a total stranger spent his time helping me. He didn't coddle me; he told me the truth I needed to hear. Once again, I was being asked to step up and take responsibility for my choices and to give up my role as a victim.

The next day, Jim went to a twelve-step meeting for alcoholics and hasn't had a drink since. That was over twenty-five years ago now. Suddenly, I didn't have anyone to drink with. Jim drank so much that I honestly didn't recognize I had a drinking problem. There was no way I was going to have a drink in front of him and jeopardize his sobriety, so I white knuckled it, denied there was an issue, and got started working the steps in my own program.

Lo and behold, when I was writing out my fourth step, a pattern evolved. Every single time I wrote down anything that I was ashamed of, felt guilty about, or regretted, I noted that I had been drunk when it happened! It slowly dawned on me that I might have a drinking problem. With that revelation I began to remember people in my past who had voiced their concern about the amount I drank—like John Kosanke, one of the owners of The Players Tennis and Racquetball Club that I managed, who was bold enough and who cared enough to tell me the truth.

I went to a different twelve-step group for alcoholics than my husband, and I, too, have now been sober for over a quarter of a century. In no other area of my life have I seen a greater positive or more immediate improvement in every area of my life than what happened when I made the choice to quit drinking. With the alcohol gone, I didn't say as many things I regretted. I didn't have guilt and remorse about not being available for my children. I didn't have to wonder what I'd done the night before that I might need to apologize for. I wasn't trying to cover up stuff that was left undone or done wrong because of my drinking. Life was profoundly less complicated.

One of the unexpected perks of not drinking was that I no longer avoided spending time with my parents. Jim and I had often opted out of their invitations to have a meal because we preferred to have cocktails before dinner, during dinner, and after dinner, and my parents didn't drink. Mom and Dad were shocked to learn that I had become an alcoholic. When I told my mother she actually responded with, "No, you're not! I've never even seen you drink!" Oh, how I wish it had been that simple.

Two points need to be crystal clear: First, I couldn't see that I had a problem until I quit focusing on my husband's problem. I had to look at me and my part in my misery. Second, I made two scary new choices that changed many, many things in my life for the better.

Admitting that there was a problem, then going outside for help changed the lives of everyone in our family for the better. Somebody had to take action and break the pattern. I honestly felt like I was going to die the night I told my husband I was going to a twelve-step meeting for family members and friends of alcoholics.

I was so afraid. We'd talked and yelled, cried and lied, wept and carried on about the problem off and on for over two years, but it took "doing" something different to instigate change.

Quitting drinking was just the beginning. Sobriety is not so much the state of not drinking as it is how one thinks about and perceives life. Sobriety is actually more of an attitude than a condition. If not drinking was all it took to straighten out lives, a lot more people would be successful at staying sober. It is the things that are broken inside of us that drive us to self-medicate. Fixing what is broken is not possible when the mind is dulled and altered chemically.

Today I know I was trying to avoid the painful consequences of my choices, and I began to drink for relief from my emotions. When I stopped the alcohol consumption, I learned that I had an almost overwhelming desire to "run away" from anything that stressed me. I was practically incapable of dealing with feeling anxious, and I still occasionally get those frantic internal feelings when I momentarily forget that God's power and strength— not mine—will see me through.

When I first quit drinking, I had fantasies of running away from my family and not having any responsibility for anyone but myself. I suddenly felt desperate for someone, anyone, to take care of me, and I was aching from the stress of trying to take care of my children and husband when I was barely surviving myself.

Jim was blessed with a complete removal of the compulsion to drink from the moment he admitted he was an alcoholic and decided to stop. I had urges to drink for over a year after I quit drinking, and each thought of a drink made me run to a meeting. Learning to live with my feelings, especially the negative ones, was difficult but doable with the help of friends who also suffered and, of course, the grace of God. Learning to communicate with my children and husband without the crutch of alcohol... now that was another deal entirely.

CHAPTER NINE

REALITY-BASED LIVING

❧

FINDING THE WAY

Life felt raw and awkward when I gave up my "dirty Coke"—the name I gave to my favorite alcoholic beverage: Diet Coke and Jack Daniel's whiskey. My kids regularly grabbed a quick drink out of my glass in passing, and Coke looks the same with or without Jack Daniel's in it, so I warned them off of the spiked Coke with a quick "No, that's dirty Coke!"

I wasn't the only one feeling awkward without dirty Coke in my life. The children have told me that their lives changed dramatically when we sobered up because they had gotten used to doing pretty much anything and everything they wanted to do. Apparently, after we'd been drinking awhile we'd forget to check on them. They felt watched and self-conscious when we were suddenly not only aware of what was going on, but interested.

Many of the freedoms they had assumed while we were otherwise disposed were lost, and Jim and I began holding them accountable for the first time in our marriage.

When we first got sober, I know I hyper-focused on the children. I realized they had been neglected, and Jim and I were trying to figure out how to navigate our parenting as a team. Previously, we had seldom had tough discussions without having had at least a few drinks. Approaching difficult topics without the buffer of alcohol to take the emotions down a notch was a new and extremely uncomfortable experience we avoided at all costs.

Jim went to his group meetings and I went to mine. We discussed neutral stuff about the children and the goings-on in the house, but our relationship and his relationship with the children were not up for discussion.

People with addictive personalities tend to replace one addiction with another. Jim filled the empty space that alcohol used to fill with group meetings three and even four times a day, which I know he needed. When that leveled off a little, he became a Bible hound. He spent every free minute reading his Bible and soaking up the truth of God's Word. I felt utterly conflicted because I was glad he was studying the Bible, but I felt as ignored as I had when he was passed out drunk. Somehow I felt doubly guilty about being jealous of his time spent in the Bible.

When Jim graduated from constant Bible reading, he moved on to learning new computer programs. From there, model trains entered his life. Everything Jim became interested in absorbed him completely. I felt lonelier after he got sober than before he'd gotten sober. At least when we were both drinking we had one thing in common, and we could talk conversationally when we were under the influence.

Over the years I filled my time and my heart with our children, my new friends, my job at the race track, then college, my horse, and eventually working with my father editing his books. Jim and I got counseling at my insistence every now and then, but nothing ever changed in the way our relationship worked.

I'll always remember the counseling session when Jim told the counselor that he was sure I'd leave him one day because of our twelve-year age difference, so he didn't want to get too invested in me emotionally. The counselor was incredulous! He told Jim that by withholding his love he was going to eventually force me to leave him. Jim was subconsciously doing what it would take to make his belief come true.

GOD MAKES EVERYTHING BETTER

At least we were on better footing with God individually. The twelve-step program we were in encouraged us to develop a relationship of total dependence on God, and our faith had grown. We had gone to a few different churches, but eventually we found the one that felt like home—Highland Meadows Christian Church in Grapevine, Texas. The people who went there had close, intimate relationships with Jesus, and they were warm and welcoming to us.

Their lives were a reflection of their beliefs and we followed their example and got involved in the Bible studies, Sunday school, and other activities. I'd never belonged to a church that had so many mature Christians who wanted to help in any way they could.

I had come to a place in my life where I knew I didn't want a divorce. I could see that I was married to a good man who loved his children and probably loved me, but was afraid to show it. I loved my kids and my in-laws, and I knew God didn't want divorce for us, so I convinced myself that I could be content even if my relationship with Jim never improved. We were strangers living in the same house, but I had God and friends I could count on to take care of my emotional needs. Compared to how things had been when I was drinking, I was happy and content. I was willing to settle for what we had.

Added Stress

Seven years into our marriage, my self-employed, entrepreneurial, be-your-own boss husband agreed to help my dad out by being the temporary president/CEO of The Zig Ziglar Corporation. That "temporary" position lasted six years, and though neither of us realized it at the time, his position caused our relationship to become even more estranged. Jim felt that he couldn't discuss his work frustrations with me because he didn't want to say anything about my family that might upset me. Almost all of my family worked together. Jim also deeply loves my father and didn't have the heart to tell Dad he needed to quit, but the strain of working with family nine-to-five was taking its toll. Jim seemed to disappear further and further into himself.

BOS

There was one especially bright spot for Jim in working in the family business and that was getting to work with my sister Suzan. Suzan and Jim had a wacky, silly, funny, ongoing, one-up, pull-one-over-on-you relationship. Their senses of humor were perfectly aligned, and nothing delighted either of them more than getting the last big laugh.

Suzan, her husband, Chad, and Jim had lunch together most days. Jim is famous for spilling his food on his tie and shirt. One day Suzan surprised Jim with his very own adult-sized bib, complete with a food-catching pocket to keep his pants clean as well. Then she made sure he didn't forget to take it with him whenever they went out. Her practical, tongue-in-cheek solution to his problem also made him look like a goofball, but that didn't stop Jim Norman from proudly wearing the bib. He figured Suzan and Chad would be embarrassed to be seen with him while he was wearing the bib, so he kept it up! Anything for that last laugh!

The day Jim got a welcome letter from AARP addressed to "Big Old Jim Norman" he knew Suzan had been at it again. Jim affectionately called her BOS (pronounced Boz) for Big Old Suzan. All of us loved the shenanigans Suzan and Jim got into and the laughter they brought to the office.

Nobody saw it more than I, but there was a little light inside my husband that went dark the day my sister died (which I'll talk about in the next chapter). She was his true friend and I loved their special friendship. Grief visited itself on all of us, but losing Suzan took Jim and me even deeper into our individual spaces as we mourned separately. We coexisted, but happiness was difficult to find in our home.

THE LAST STRAW

The Internet had come to the Norman household, and I was concerned that an old addiction Jim had overcome before I ever met him might reappear. He assured me he wouldn't have any problems, and I hoped he was right.

I'm sure it started innocently enough, but I wasn't prepared to deal with Jim's problem when it reappeared. I couldn't live in our house and pretend that everything was okay. I had settled for the mask of a marriage already. I wasn't prepared to be miserable at the same time.

Our renters had recently moved out of our second home, so I started making arrangements to separate from Jim. I also called Randy Snyder, our pastor, for an appointment. I wanted to do what was right by God, and I didn't know what our new church's stance was on divorce. I think I wanted permission to divorce, and I was pretty sure I'd get it after I told our pastor the truth about our marriage and all that was going on.

Boy, oh boy, did I ever make my case! I walked into the pastor's office with eleven years of hurt and disappointment rolling off my tongue. I wrapped it all up by saying I didn't know my new church's stance on divorce, but I wanted one, and I wanted to know what he had to say about it. I was tired of going to counselors, I was tired of being lonely, and I was tired of hoping things would get better. I was just flat out of hope.

When I finally quit talking, my pastor told me the church felt divorce was only acceptable in a very few instances and none of what I had described qualified. He said God could heal broken marriages, and he was going to ask me to do one thing— just one thing—before I went and filed for divorce. Randy said, "Just once, will you and Jim meet with Ken Bryant, our associate pastor, who is also a marriage counselor?"

I sure didn't want to, but I agreed, and Randy called Ken in to set up the time with me. I hadn't even told Jim that I was planning on leaving him, so I decided I would tell him while we were in our session with Ken.

A few evenings later Jim and I arrived at Ken's office in the church. He spoke with us separately and then together. My husband denied that he was having problems with his old habit, and I explained that I had visited the sites he had been spending time on and knew what he was up to. Then Jim admitted that he had been struggling, but had been convicted at church and had quit the offending behavior two weeks earlier. I said I didn't believe him.

"If Jim can prove that he has already stopped his undesirable behavior, will you consider trying to work out the other marriage problems?" Ken asked. I said that I would, confident that I wouldn't have to because I was positive he had not stopped his behavior.

Then the most amazing thing happened. Ken asked if he could call on a member of the church who was an expert on computers and ask him to meet us at our house. Ken assured me that this man could tell by looking at files in our computer if what Jim said was true. In all of my years of going to church, never had a church member been willing to come out at nine p.m. to help perfect strangers. This was a level of church fellowship I'd never experienced, and I came to value and cherish this very practical brotherly love.

By two o'clock the next morning my sheepish husband had been proven truthful. He had stopped cruising the Internet, and while I was relieved, I was still determined to move out. We had tried many, many times to fix our marriage, but after a few months it always went back to being the "same-old, same-old." I believed that we might get more accomplished in separate households, and in the event nothing changed, I would already be out of the house. Yes, I had my skeptical, doubting plan for potential failure in place, but I was willing to take a wait-and-see attitude one more time.

God's Plans

Pain and struggle bring wisdom and force focus. They shuffle the deck of life so that what really matters comes to the top of the stack. Then the hand you're dealt reveals your ace in the hole, and once again, God trumps all.

I marvel often at the finesse God uses to orchestrate His

masterful plan. When we separated, Jim no longer worked at the family business, a blessing that revealed itself with time. I went from working on an hourly basis as my father's editor to a salaried position, which also proved to be a blessing that was revealed with time.

Jim and I saw Ken Bryant once a week individually for several months and concentrated on forging a closer walk with God. Ken taught us what marriage commitment really is and what God intended for our roles to be within the marriage.

During that time, though we lived in separate houses, we managed to see each other for a few minutes a day when I'd drop our dog off to Jim so she wouldn't be lonely while I worked an extra night job waiting tables to help make ends meet. It was strange to feel a little shy and out of place around my husband, but we were both tentative and unsure of what would come next.

I know some people think being separated is a license to date other people, but Jim and I had grown enough in our faith to recognize that our marriage was still intact and neither one of us would have dated other people during our separation, even if we were just waiting for our divorce to be final.

Our three oldest children, all of whom were adults by the time of our separation, believed we'd get back together and actually seemed unaffected by our separation. Amey, our youngest, was the most upset, and she very much wanted me to go through with the divorce. She was angry because it didn't seem to her that Jim was working very hard to restore the marriage. When she learned that we were getting counseling and working on the relationship, she asked me why I didn't just get it over with. I told her that I married Jim "for better or worse," and this was just the "worse" part. We talked about vows before God, His covenants, and why those were enough reason to try to make it work.

The whole time Jim and I were separated there was only one person beyond our church fellowship who told me God could heal my marriage. She wasn't even someone I knew very well, but she pulled me aside after a meeting one night and told me that her separation from her husband was the best thing that had ever happened to them. She said they lived in separate households for several months, but now that they'd been reunited, they were happier than ever before.

Just that one woman encouraged me to keep trying. I don't know why so many people seem so eager to support the death of a marriage. We all know that we carry our problems with us, as in "wherever I go, there I am." While first marriages have a 50 percent chance of failing, second marriages have a 67 percent chance of failing.*

It is actually shocking to me when I hear anyone explain that the reason for their divorce is as simple as, "We've grown in different directions." Or, "We were so young, we didn't really know enough about what we wanted in a spouse. We fell out of love. That old spark just isn't there anymore." Those things can be fixed with work, with effort, with commitment, with God.

I can talk about divorce because I've experienced one. Even though I wanted my first marriage to end, I was not prepared for

---

* Jennifer Baker, Director of Post-Graduate Program in Marriage and Family Therapy at Forest Institute of Professional Psychology in Springfield, Missouri.

the grief, the depression, and the remorse I felt when it was over. I mourned the death of my marriage for years after the divorce. It was the death of a dream, an ideal, and the end of a live-in relationship for my daughter with her father. As I said earlier, divorce stinks, even when you honestly believe you need one.

When Jim and I separated, we used the space and distance to work out our misunderstandings. That is what we suffered from. We tried to read each other's minds, we couldn't let go of our preconceived notions about what the other was thinking or feeling, and we could not communicate without the white noise of our internal conversations convincing us that we were miles apart in every area of our lives. My husband once said our marriage was as dead as Lazarus, and like Lazarus, it has been raised from the dead.

I thank God for the one woman who gave me a seed of hope. I could see how truly happy she was, and I wanted that for me, for my husband, and for my children. After six months of individual counseling with Ken, we began counseling together as a couple, learning how to communicate, and after a year of separation, we happily combined our households for all time.

For over seventeen years now I have had the kind of marriage others desire for themselves, and though it is hard to imagine, I have it with a guy on whom I'd nearly given up. I was so "over him" when we split up, but I discovered that Jim Norman is the most amazing and wonderful husband. I adore this man to pieces and can't fathom life without him—my confidant, my soul mate, my earthly joy. My gratitude for God's unwillingness to allow me to settle for the marriage I had overwhelms me at every thought of what we would have missed.

If you will surrender trying to fix your spouse and get to work on fixing your relationship with God, you will become the mate God always intended your spouse to have. And when you are that person, your spouse will respond in kind.

God can fix anything you give over entirely to Him. I was learning that fact, but I was still unwilling to go to Him with my deepest, darkest past, much less dwell on it myself.

CHAPTER TEN

LOSING SUZAN

PART OF LIFE

I can't go a page farther without writing about what losing my sister Suzan meant to me in the scope of growing up Ziglar. Nothing that happened before or since has had a more profound impact on my life, or my parents' lives.

As I mentioned in the last chapter, losing Suzan initially increased the distance my husband and I kept from one another, but in a roundabout way contributed to us establishing a happy, fulfilling, godly, faith-based marriage. God really can and does fix anything you give over entirely to Him. It's true that our family didn't have a choice about my sister dying, but recognizing that Suzan had always been God's child and that she was only meant to be on this earth for a period of time made it possible for us to release our human desires and accept God's plan for "fixing" Suzan—regardless of how He might choose to do that. The ability to trust God that much is a picture of the peace that passes understanding. Praise God our family had that peace.

In the twenty years I've been Dad's editor, the hardest book we've ever worked on together was *Confessions of a Grieving Christian.* Dad was inspired to write that book because he wanted his readers to know how God, friends, and family were helping him walk his way through the grief of losing his eldest daughter, Suzan, to pulmonary fibrosis. He wanted his readers to know that there is joy in the midst of grief, and he knew people would wonder how "Mr. Positive" was dealing with his devastating loss. He wanted to be transparent. There is no easy way around grief, but he felt if he could put into words what he was going through and how God worked it out in his life, he might be able to help others in their grief journey.

It had also occurred to all of us that *Confessions of a Grieving Christian* would be an exclamation point for *Confessions of a Happy Christian,* an earlier book he had written specifically for my then-agnostic sister Suzan. He wrote that book praying that Suzan would read it, see his joy in Jesus Christ, and accept Him as her Lord and Savior, which, thankfully, she eventually did.

My sister Suzan turned forty-six years old on May 10, 1995, three days before she died. We are all grateful that she did not suffer the long, drawn-out, bedridden end that is typical of pulmonary fibrosis, but her sudden decline took all of us by surprise. One day she was at work, the next she was in the hospital.

We all knew her condition was terminal unless she got a lung transplant, but we thought she was at least two or three years away from needing one. The first week she was in the hospital she was put on life support, so drugs were used to keep her in a semi-comatose state. Before the week was out doctors told us that she was too weak to survive a lung transplant, and mega doses of steroids were the only thing left to try. She wasn't expected to live through the weekend, but the steroids caused her to rally.

For a few days they let her come out of the drug-induced coma enough to nod yes and no answers, but they were never able to wean her off the respirator. Eventually, her organs began to fail, and we knew we were losing her.

A great deal of grieving went on the two weeks before Suzan died. Dad struggled with his speaking schedule. Should he go? Should he stay? His optimism and his denial told him Suzan would be fine and he should go. His family feared that he wouldn't forgive himself if she died before he could return. We talked about the dilemma amongst ourselves. We knew Dad had always dealt with stressful situations by praying, trusting God, and staying fully occupied.

Each of us clung to the hope that prayer might turn her circumstances around and that God might grant us a miracle, but Suz herself had said in earlier discussions about her prognosis that God was sovereign and if He chose to heal her by taking her home to heaven, that was His prerogative. She even asked Dad to resist his natural inclination to look on the positive side. She asked him not to assure her children that prayer would heal their mother. She reminded Dad that we had no way of knowing what God would do, and she didn't want her daughters mad at God if He didn't restore her health.

By Friday, May 12, we called Dad to come home and sent another speaker to take his place. We were asking Suzan to hang on—telling her that Dad was on his way back and to hold on so he could see her again before she left. She wasn't able to respond, but we had been told she could hear us.

Her doctor let us know the end was near, and we wept and waited. We talked about stuff that wasn't related and stuff that was. We laughed at things that weren't funny and moments that were, and wondered how laughter could come under such tragic circumstances. We even ate all of the chocolate-covered cherries our family friend, Paula Reed, had brought to Suzan. Nothing seemed real.

How should I act, what could I say, what should I do while I waited for one of the most significant people in my life to leave me forever? I couldn't breathe in her essence deeply enough to capture it for a lifetime without her. I couldn't hold on tightly enough that I would never have to let go. It was impossible to pray more earnestly than I had already prayed, so I chanted my endless "I love yous," and waited through the deep darkness that led to her last breath, her last heartbeat, and the end of my time with her on earth.

My sister Cindy and I were with her when her numbers started to drop. The beeps on the heart monitor got farther apart, and her oxygen levels were going down when the nurse said to get anyone who wanted to be with her when she died. I ran to the waiting room where Mom and Dad (who had arrived in time) and other members of the family were visiting with friends and told them to hurry.

We were all brokenhearted as we stood helplessly by her bed. We knew she was gone before the nurse stated that harsh fact. We could feel that she had left even as the heart line went flat. The unimaginable, the unthinkable, had come to pass. Suzan was gone. How could that be? Our minds could hardly grasp the concept...gone. What does that mean, really? *Gone.*

None of us had ever lost someone so close. I knew my parents had just lost their child—that was harder for me than the fact that I had just lost my sister. My heart could not conceive of that kind of grief, and I struggled with my own sadness...all-consuming, palpable, and black.

There was nothing left to do in the hospital, no reason to stay, so each of us left the building we'd worn like a funeral shroud for two long weeks and went where we were needed. Emotional and physical exhaustion had to be pushed to the side for a bit longer... funeral plans had to be made.

The first time I saw my father after we all left the hospital was the next morning. I was slowing at a stop sign on the way to his house when I caught sight of him walking on the sidewalk ahead of me. His head was bent forward and his shoulders were heaving up and down with sobs that racked his whole body. He looked so vulnerable and heartbroken that I couldn't get to him fast enough. I drove a little ahead of him, threw the car into PARK, and jumped out in time to catch him up into my hug. There were no words for the moment. We held each other and cried. I got back in the car and went to his house to be with Mom, and he walked on, doing what God had clearly told him he should do—walk and pray and cry. Over the months that followed, I came upon that scene time and again, but I didn't stop, knowing he was walking through his grief and God was walking with him.

THE WHY QUESTION

The day after Suzan died, I had gone to the grocery store for supplies for Suzan's house and it happened to be Mother's Day. Everywhere I looked there were signs advertising Mother's Day gifts, cards, and special ways to remember mothers. There were the corsages with the red flowers to be worn by females whose mother was still living, and white corsages to be worn by those whose mother had died. It hit me like a ton of bricks that my fifteen-year-old niece Katherine was too young, way too young, to be wearing a white one. And then I thought how bittersweet Mother's Day had instantly become for my own mother. In that moment of reckoning I had a full dose of life being not fair. And because of this I had to take the natural little seeds of doubt that had crept into my mind and heart to my Maker, so that my faith could be restored.

I grieved on the back of my paint mare Rosie. I tried not to cry in front of Jim too much. He was having such a hard time himself and we weren't close at the time so I didn't go to him for comfort. Riding my mare through the woods, by the lake, and across the fields took me to God's sanctuary where I could commune with Him and remember Suzan with unchecked tears.

Suzan is gone, but she is not missing...we know where she is.

She has an everlasting home. As Jim Lewis, Suzan's pastor, said at her funeral, "In the past few days you may have read that Suzan Witmeyer died on May 13, 1995. DON'T YOU BELIEVE IT! She is more alive than she has ever been."

THE GATHERING

True to tradition, our close friends and family gathered together for a shared meal and a time of visiting after Suzan's funeral. There were probably over two hundred people who came and went during the next three to four hours, and there was one recurring theme. Remark after remark was made about the peace our family had, the obvious love and affection we shared, and the total agreement that God was in control. As a family, our faith was visible to those who came to comfort us.

In the days leading up to Suzan's passing, many remarks were made by the hospital staff and even other families in the ICU waiting room that our family had a closeness and faith rarely seen. By God's grace we were able to have moments of joy and laughter in the midst of our grief and pain. We were grateful that we didn't have to struggle with questions about Suzan's faith and that we all understood that if she died, she'd be in a far better place than we were. We wanted what was best for Suzan, and we trusted that God would see that she had the best.

Dad's favorite Scripture, "And we know that all things work together for good to them that love God, to them who are the called according to his purpose" (Romans 8:28 KJV), helped us see the good that came with our Father welcoming Suzan home.

Part of that good was a result of the way my husband, Jim, handled his emotions during the time Suzan was in the ICU. The thoughts and observations he penned in his journal about how our family dealt with crisis have touched many, many people since Dad decided to use what Jim had written in his book *Confessions of a Grieving Christian.*

Each of us in the immediate family developed an even closer walk with God. Friends told us they saw the importance of a close church family because of the way Mom and Dad's church, Prestonwood Baptist, and Plano Bible Church, Suzan and Chad's church, ministered to them, both at the hospital and in their homes. Jim and I stepped up our search for a church home because of what we witnessed, and that is when we found Highland Meadows Christian Church, where the members of the fellowship helped us save our marriage just fourteen months later.

Jim was earnestly praying for Suzan while she was in ICU, and he said it hit him that he was praying for a woman who was dying of a lung disease and then he'd go outside the hospital to smoke. He felt like a fake, so he promised God he'd quit smoking when Suzan left the hospital, regardless of whether she lived or not. After his promise to God, he was able to pray in peace. Jim has not had a cigarette since the day after Suzan's funeral.

Another blessing for us was that the staff at St. Paul Hospital had experienced Zig Ziglar Customer Service training in the years before Suzan was admitted to their hospital. Suzan was given top-notch care, and we were beneficiaries of what they learned. They also told us how much it touched them to see my father living out what he said they should do in their own lives.

One of Suzan's lifelong friends gave her life to Jesus because of the testimony she heard others saying about how Suzan's life changed when she accepted Jesus Christ as her Lord and Savior. The examples of Romans 8:28 at work are nearly endless.

Today, almost seventeen years later, it is well with our souls. We miss her deeply; we have all discovered that the grief becomes bearable with time, but the feeling of loss and a degree of grief will always be with us. There was one Scripture that especially helped all of us deal with the fact that Suzan died young: Isaiah 57:1, "The righteous perish, and no one ponders it in his heart; devout men are taken away, and no one understands that the righteous are taken away to be spared from evil" (NIV). We believed God spared Suzan from something we don't even want to fathom.

New Insight

Suzan wasn't able to tell us what was going on spiritually as her body began to fail, but I believe I can tell you a little about what she was possibly seeing because of my precious friend and next-door neighbor, Mr. Hubert Lee Boner. In August of 2004, God gave me a ringside seat to heaven when I had the blessing of visiting with my dying friend, Mr. Boner, a man I thought of as my grandfather. At the time, I couldn't understand why I was being allowed to witness how thin the veil between this world and the next truly is, but enough time has passed for me to see how the experience strengthened my faith and allowed me to comfort and encourage others.

I adored Mr. Boner; he was a great teacher of life and he loved Jesus with every fiber of his being. Mr. Boner always had a big garden, and he'd call me over to visit with him while he hoe-chopped weeds or picked vegetables, and he'd preach to me about Peter and Jesus. He loved the apostle Peter and related to him because Peter seemed to mess things up and then have to get right with Jesus once again, just like he did.

Mr. Boner lived a life that reflected his Lord and Savior, even as he battled with cancer. As the days passed and he became bedridden, I began to visit him in his living room where the most wonderful hospice workers in the universe had set up his hospital bed. For three long weeks hospice kept watch twenty-four hours a day, an unusually long period of time, and in the end Mr. Boner's volunteers were all praying they would be the one with him when he went to live with his King.

Almost every day that Mr. Boner lingered on, something amazing would happen. It was so astounding that I wrote down everything he said so that I could remember it always. The first thing he confided was, "Julie, I'm seeing things I've never seen before. Everything will be explained." Usually, what he said would be somewhat of an announcement...it'd just come out of the blue like, "Julie, everything is going to be all right. I'm okay." Or, "Julie, are you happy?" I replied, "Yes sir, I'm very happy." He said, "I'm happy too." Many of the things he said would not be significant under normal conditions, but they were huge in the face of death.

During Mr. Boner's last week, I was helping the nurse try to make him as comfortable as possible by raising or lowering the bed. After we'd adjusted his position again, he held his arm up and gestured in a sweeping motion across the whole room as he said, "Look at all the people—so many people all around. I'm ready to go. I feel bad. I'm ready. I want to go."

That same week a hospice nurse named Judy told me that when Mr. Boner awoke he saw something above his head. She said his face was filled with wonder and awe, and his head turned this way and that as he followed the movements of what he was seeing in the air across the whole of the room. When Judy asked him what he was seeing, he immediately turned toward her, patted her arm, and said, "It's not for you to know."

A little while after Judy had shared her experience, Mr. Boner's face lit up again, but he just looked upward. I asked what he was looking at, expecting the same words in reply, but he said in a reverent tone, "My house." I asked, "What does it look like, Mr. Boner?" And in a hushed whisper, full of awe, he said, "It's beautiful. It's so beautiful." And he continued to stare, enraptured, for quite some time.

The last clearly audible thing Mr. Boner said in front of me was when he raised his right arm, looked deeply toward what I could not see, and pled, "Take my hand. I'm ready to go. Come and get me."

Mr. Boner showed me that God prepares the way, and that the veil between this world and the next grows thin so we can see that what is to come is so much more than what is left behind.

God prepares our hearts and makes us ready to be with Him. Any fear of the unknown is washed away, and as Mr. Boner said, "Everything will be explained."

One Sad but Accepting Family

My father and mother both set a beautiful example of a godly man and woman in mourning. They trusted God. They accepted that Suzan was where God had determined it would be best for her to be.

Dad openly, unashamedly, mourned the loss of my sister. He wept at the sight of any blond-headed little girl, the strains of his favorite hymns, the reading of meaningful Scripture, and the kind and consoling words of friends. The searing pain of her absence struck his heart.

We all wept. Even with our total faith in God, losing Suzan presented a new and difficult journey for our family. Today I count it a beautiful privilege to mourn, to have loved enough to be brokenhearted. Our family desires to comfort others with the comfort that has been extended to us. Because Christ lives, we can face tomorrow, and when our tomorrows are over? Well, we already know the home He has gone ahead to prepare for us is "beautiful, so beautiful."

CHAPTER ELEVEN

ALVORD, TEXAS!

NEW BEGINNINGS IN A BEAUTIFUL PLACE

We topped the hill and practically swooned at the view. The Alvordian Valley was lush and green as far as the eye could see. Our earlier trips had been in the dark of night when stars peppered the sky and the lights of the big city faded with each mile we drove north. We were on the hunt for a new home, a new style of living, and practically giddy to be in love with each other once again. Honestly, we felt like we had our whole lives ahead of us.

Our children were all grown and living on their own, and our reason for staying in the overcrowded suburbs of Dallas-Ft. Worth had ceased to exist. Jim worked for himself as a business consultant, and I could edit Dad's books from anywhere as long as we had a good Internet connection. The only negative about our new plan was leaving Highland Meadows Christian Church and finding a new church home, but we had faith God would put us in exactly the right place.

I'm often asked what possessed us to move to Alvord. Alvord

has about a thousand residents and no apparent zoning laws. It is rural America. A 350,000-dollar house sits on a lot between two mobile homes. Condemned houses stand for years before they are bulldozed down and carted off, or until the volunteer fire department burns them down so they can practice putting out fires. Alvord has character!

Right after we moved to town, I called city hall to find out if there were any ordinances against owning swine within the city limits. I thought I might want a miniature Vietnamese pot-bellied pig. The lady who answered the phone laughed herself to the point of tears as she tried to tell me between her snorting and hooting and hollerin' that Alvord didn't have any ordinances. She knew right away another city slicker had moved into town. I felt a strange mixture of excitement and fear about the apparent freedoms we were about to experience.

I have come to love Alvord because of people like Roy King and his wife, Lori. Roy owns the Alvord Farm Supply store where I buy my horse feed and where we take our grandkids to see the geese and to pet baby goats. Lori opened a boutique called Reflections where you can get your hair cut and colored, sell your old gold, spend some time in one of the tanning beds, or shop for really cute clothes, shoes, and amazing jewelry. When you're done there you can walk half a block to the first yellow blinking light in town and get great home cookin' at K.T.'s Café. We don't have any stop lights yet, and we hope we don't get any, ever.

Our interest in Alvord began with my discovery of the improved horse trails on the LBJ National Grasslands. I can haul my horse eight minutes up the road and ride over one hundred miles of beautiful trails through pine forests, hardwood forests, the plains full of native grasses, across ancient ocean floors on towering plateaus, and through deep gorges. Jim and I rode together for the first few years until a bad horse wreck convinced Jim he'd had enough of horseback riding. Now I ride with my girlfriends, and Jim sticks to riding his tractor—it doesn't buck.

We got involved in the community, took up square dancing, made new friends, and found the church I mentioned at the beginning of this book. The pastor and the body of believers in our new church home, Believer's International Fellowship—a nondenominational Bible church—taught me how to live for Jesus. Until then I had been learning how to love and trust Jesus. Now I was finding out that my life truly wasn't any of my business! In fact, I exist for God's pleasure and glory, not the other way around.

Gene Smith, our pastor, told us on a regular basis that he'd know he was doing a good job preaching if he came to church one Sunday and nobody was there because we were all out doing what God had put in front of us to do. Gene wanted us to be *doers*—"But be ye doers of the word, and not hearers only, deceiving your own selves" (James 1:22 KJV).

I learned that being obedient to do what God has in front of me begins with making myself available and willing to do as I am asked. I've found that what God puts on my heart seldom comes at a "convenient" time. We're all busy. I'm busy. Life interrupts our busyness at the most inopportune times. I am reminded of the Scripture, Hebrews 13:2, "Do not forget to entertain strangers, for by so doing some people have entertained angels without knowing it" (NIV).

More and more I find that I am stopped in my tracks by strangers needing help on the highway between Alvord and our nearest town with a Walmart—Decatur, Texas. I have been blessed with every incident, and the joy of helping is mine. The blessing outweighs the inconvenience every single time. Interruptions like that, though, are small and easy to be obedient about.

I am, however, no Pollyanna! I have to take myself to the "woodshed" (ask God to forgive me) on a way too regular basis. Or to the "cabin" (a place I go to be alone with God) for some spiritual restoration when I get too far out of line—and it always involves me getting the impression that I suddenly ought to have some say in my life. I get all gripey and whiney and complain about how I don't want to go to Nineveh, and I don't care that Jonah didn't want to do what he was asked either...I just want my way. The resulting misery isn't worth the self-expression.

Missy's Dream

It was late in the summer of 2005 when Missy said she had a dream about me the night before and that I was supposed to do the thing that I'd been asked to do and that God couldn't fully use me until I had done it.

I groaned inwardly. I knew the jig was up. It was time to deal with the dregs of my past. Even in this, I would be obedient.

I left church, went home, and called my sister Cindy. "Sign me up for that counseling," I said.

"You're kidding! I thought you were swamped with that book deadline and there was no way you were going to try to deal with this. What changed your mind?" Cindy asked. I told her about Missy's dream. Within a matter of weeks we were both on a difficult but life-altering journey of healing. Over a quarter century of regret, shame, guilt, grief, pain, and depression was about to be put to rest.

SORROWS AND BLESSINGS

For years I fought the memory of two precious little ones. I had hardened my heart to the reality of their existence when I aborted them, and I feared that if I ever let my thoughts dwell on those babies, I would break in two and cry myself to death. In the depths of my being I felt that if I ever really thought about what I'd done, the mourning would never end.

A lot of wrong choices went into getting me to a place where I would not only consider abortion, but go through with it without so much as a backward glance. What began with the vicious rumor of the jealous cheerleader escalated out of control as I tried desperately to fit in and belong.

I grew to hate school with a passion. My ruined reputation made me even more of an outsider, and I did eventually live up to the rumors about me. I sought out family-planning clinics to get birth control and even went to Parkland Hospital on my own to get a physical for the pill.

What were my parents doing, you ask? As I said earlier, they didn't have a clue about what I was up to, simply because I was not openly rebellious. When my sister Suzan tried to tell them I was in trouble and making lots of bad choices, they simply couldn't believe her. To them, I seemed fine.

Having raced through my teen years, I was married and divorced by the age of twenty-one.

I wasn't dating much the first few years after the divorce because I was working and taking care of my baby. When I did start dating, my inability to say no to sex surfaced again, and I hated myself even more. I hadn't started back on birth control after my divorce because I wasn't planning on being sexually active, and I wrongly thought not getting on the pill would help me say no.

I got pregnant by a man I barely knew and didn't even tell him about the baby until long after he could have influenced my decision. I was three months pregnant when I aborted the baby who would have been my second child, Winnie Beth. The receptionist at the abortion clinic asked me to bring cash. They took their part when I signed in and told me to give the rest to the abortionist when he called me into his office to talk to me. When I handed him the money, he declared, "I love stupid women like you," and he kept waving the cash at me. I could feel the hate, and considering what he did all day every day, today I understand.

I had hardened my heart. I refused to think about "the baby." Abortion was legal, and I was getting one. You'd think that having a daughter of my own would be enough to convince me that a baby is a baby, but I had bought into the idea that a fetus isn't a baby yet.

Cindy, my sister, had an abortion when she was in college, and I had always thought Mom and Dad had chosen it for her. It wasn't until our post-abortion counseling that I learned she was the one who insisted she wanted an abortion. So when I chose to have an abortion, I tried to console myself by thinking my parents would be okay with it—but in my heart I knew they wouldn't approve. Dad wasn't a Christian when Cindy had her abortion, but he was when I had mine. He was teaching the sanctuary class at First Baptist Dallas, and all I could think of was the shame I'd bring on our family. I was having a hard time supporting and caring for one child, how could I ever manage two? I justified it every way to Sunday and went alone to do the deed, even refusing the Valium the abortionist offered so I could leave the clinic sooner and drive myself home.

Right after I aborted Winnie Beth, I became profoundly depressed. For years I thought my depression had to do with a relationship that didn't work out. I lost a business that had supported me completely because I was unable to work, and I even began drinking at home.

Since my divorce I had worked jobs that allowed me to spend the most time possible with my little girl, but when looking for work after the abortion, I managed to get a job that took me away from home day and night for weeks on end, so I spent very little time with my four-year-old daughter. I didn't know it, but I was already suffering symptoms common to many women who have abortions.

A few years passed, and then I got pregnant by a successful drug addict/alcoholic, and I told myself the baby would probably be abnormal because of his habits. I knew I didn't want to marry that guy, so without telling him and within the first month, I had an abortion.

The second abortion was easier to get than the first. Because

I decided to believe that a fetus was just tissue, I also believed that the sooner I removed the tissue, the further away it was from being a real baby. Since I didn't let the pregnancy go on as long, it didn't seem as bad. Selfish, scared people can justify a lot of things. In an instant, Robert Curtis was gone. Months later I told his father what I'd done. He, like the father of Winnie Beth, offered to reimburse me for half the expense.

Over the years I got counseling, and eventually my abortions came up. I thought I had worked them through and even told Mom and Dad what I'd done. We all cried and we had a memorial service for the babies, but the deep sadness wouldn't leave, and I felt like God would never forgive me for taking their lives. I "knew," according to the Bible, that I had been forgiven for every sin, for every bad deed. But I wasn't forgiving myself for choosing not to have my babies. My choice had been selfish and purposely without a thought for my unborn children. From my human perspective, I didn't deserve to be forgiven.

My post-abortion symptoms persisted. I had suffered years of not wanting to be around babies. Baby showers made me feel miserable, and I even felt disconnected from my own grandchildren. Holding them reminded me that babies are real, and I could see, touch, and smell the sweet essence of what my babies would have become.

When my sister Cindy first invited me to attend a post-abortion group I said, "No way! I'm not going down that road again. I don't have the time or the energy." She said she had to go to get help once and for all. I didn't give it another thought...until Missy told me her dream.

When Missy said God couldn't fully use me until I'd dealt with what I had been asked to do, I knew it was time to be obedient. I hadn't done it when Cindy put it in front of me the first time, but now I saw God's hand in it, and He had my full attention.

TRANSPARENCY

I arrived at the first post-abortion session with resigned dread and a degree of fear. I knew a hornet's nest of emotions was about to be stirred up. What I didn't expect was how quickly God was going to break through the hardened wall of my heart and make it possible for me to mourn the loss of my beautiful babies.

After only a few sessions, I realized the Bible study we were doing (I am not naming the study here as I strongly believe women should not try to take this healing journey by themselves) was very spot on. It started with knowing the areas we needed to have healed, and a look into God's character. I learned that my aversion to babies was typical for women who have had abortions.

That very week a new family visited our church. They had four children of their own and they were taking care of three little children of a friend who had been displaced by Hurricane Katrina. The children's father was in Iraq and the mother had been evacuated to a hospital in Houston because of a high-risk pregnancy. The youngest child was a little boy about ten months old, and he was crying in his high chair. The husband and wife taking care of him were both busy with the other children, and all I could think as I looked across the room at that little baby crying his heart out in the high chair was, "Poor little guy, he has been ripped away from his mama. She will be in Houston for weeks yet, and he doesn't even know these folks."

My heart just broke for him. I asked if I could pick him up, and then I cradled him and walked the halls, tears streaming as I thought over this child's sudden and complete separation from his mother. After awhile he fell asleep, and as I stared into his innocent face, a deep love for the babies I had rejected awakened in my heart.

From that moment on, and for the first time since my abortions, I could see a baby and think good, happy thoughts. I no longer minded catching their eye and making them smile. I even wanted to touch and hold them and breathe in their baby-powder goodness.

I'm not sure how God is going to use me in the pro-life movement, but I am willing to go where He will take me. I believe that a woman who has come through the darkness of abortion and lived with the regret and grief can become a powerful voice against abortion when she accepts that she is forgiven. My post-abortion counseling gave me my voice back; it removed my last secret shame. The post-abortion counseling I received restored my relationship with my aborted children, my living children, and my grandchildren. It made me rightly see my position in God's eyes and freed me to speak out about the tragedy of abortion, not only for the babies, but for the women who abort them.

Women like me who overcome the four cornerstones of post-abortion syndrome (regret, guilt, shame, and depression) can speak truthfully to other women about what is never addressed at family planning clinics that promote abortion. We can attest to the fact that women who have abortions suffer greatly and unexpectedly as a result of their decision. It affects them, their families, and even the world.

I hope the transparency of my family will make a difference in the lives of women everywhere—those who haven't yet made a wrong choice as well as those who already have. I know it is difficult for those who have championed life to read what I—a perpetrator of the crime they all work so passionately to prevent—have to say, but I pray you can see how helping women in my position heal enough to be able to talk openly about their grief, regret, and pain can influence other women not to make the wrong choice and ultimately save unborn babies.

I've met women who feel bad that they don't feel worse about their abortions. I've met women who abused the babies they did have because of post-abortion syndrome. I've met women who knew they were forgiven and who did not struggle like I have, but I've met many more women who deeply regret their decision to choose death over life, and they suffer daily with the complete finality of their irreversible choice.

Today I understand that God could not fully use me with that dark cloud of shame, suppressed grief, and regret hanging over me. Until I could talk openly about my abortions, I always had something to hide, and under those circumstances anything I had to say about how wonderful my Savior is would be said without complete faith.

I am thankful that I worship a risen Savior and that He can

and does make all things right. Because of Him I can face tomorrow. Because of Him I will hold my babies in heaven. Because of post-abortion counseling I'm able to influence mothers to make the right choice. Because of post-abortion counseling I am blessed to show women who still suffer silently that their deepest, darkest secret can be faced and they can be completely healed by our heavenly Father.

The proactive counseling individuals receive about the truth of abortion saves lives. If you have been living with the burden of abortion like I did and you are tired of hurting, tired of running from the memory and the magnitude of what you've done, won't you please allow one of the many ministries available to help you restore your relationship with your aborted baby or babies and help you heal your aching heart? It may be hard to imagine, but today I have a love relationship with my little boy, Robert Curtis, and my little girl, Winnie Beth. I mourn their absence in a healthy, normal way. I miss them as if I had held them in my arms and lost them. I treasure who they are, and I anticipate seeing them in heaven. God forgives those who repent and ask for His forgiveness. His forgiveness is total. You can learn as I did that forgiving yourself and accepting what Christ has already done for you will set you free.

What I have shared has the blessing of my entire family, who want me to be bold in my testimony. I write this book in honor of my youngest daughter, Winnie Beth, and my baby boy, Robert Curtis. They live in my heart, but they reside with Jesus, and I can only imagine the joy when I finally meet them in heaven.

CHAPTER TWELVE

PIVOTAL LIFE POINT

FORGIVEN

Finally, I got it. I understood. How could I accept forgiveness for an act I wasn't even able to think about, much less acknowledge the part I played in it? How could I approach the throne of God when I could not yet look in the face of my child? Until I could own my sin, own my grief, own my loss, and accept that not only did I kill my unborn children, I broke the heart of God, I could not repent and ask for forgiveness.

It broke my heart to acknowledge that my babies existed and that I had rejected, destroyed, and thrown them away like so much trash. It broke my heart to understand how I broke God's heart. Who was that frightened girl, so disconnected from her soul that she could do such a thing? Who was that woman who didn't and wouldn't trust God for anything? I learned the answers to those questions during my post-abortion counseling, and the answers came straight out of the Bible!

Today I know you can get past your past, but you have to go through it to get beyond it! You don't have to understand the *why* of everything, but you must understand the WHO of God! Knowing who God is, what His character is, who He says He is, and who you are in relationship to Him will absolutely change your life and your choices.

SECRETS

Back when I was getting sober, I learned that people are "only as sick as their secrets." The more secrets a person has, the harder it is to live a well-adjusted, problem-free life. Secrets equal shame, and shame exists in the continuation of the behavior and the absence of forgiveness. My paternal grandmother used to say, "Tell the truth and tell it ever, costeth what it will, for he who hides the wrong he did, does the wrong thing still."

Until I dealt with my abortions I did not know how seriously they impacted my life. I did not know that I was spiritually hogtied with the shame and regret of what I'd done. I didn't have a clue that my secret kept me from being used by God for His glory, for His purpose, and for His pleasure. I was willing to serve God; I just didn't know what He wanted me to do other than get to know Him better. When Missy told me God couldn't fully use me until I'd done what He had asked me to do, I willingly did as He asked.

After I finished my post-abortion counseling, I asked my pastor if I could share with our fellowship the spiritual healing I'd received and the joy of restoration I'd experienced. All of the

shame was gone; only the joy that is Jesus remained. The freedom to love my aborted children, to grieve the loss of them, to
anticipate seeing them in heaven, is a miracle, and I had to share
it with my church family.

Several months after our sessions ended, my sister Cindy and
I were blessed to speak for five minutes at the fundraiser dinner
for the Real Choices Pregnancy Center where we received our
post-abortion counseling, and in February of 2009 I was hon-
ored to share my story at a Real Choices fundraising luncheon
with both of my parents in attendance.

The Support of Parents

My parents are amazing! They were born in the 1920s, in the era
where family secrets were kept secret. You just didn't discuss "private business." Hearing my story breaks their hearts, and yet there
my eighty-plus-year-old parents sat, crying when I cried, laughing when I laughed, and shooting love beams at me every single
second. They support my sister and me, and they want women to
know the truth about the pain and devastation caused by abortion.

When Cindy and I told Mom and Dad we were getting more
help in dealing with our abortions and how the post-abortion program we were in was helping us deal with our pain and grief, Daddy
was extremely moved. Through the years he had told Cindy many
times how deeply he regretted letting her get her abortion. With
tears streaming down his face he said, "Maybe this is my purpose.
Maybe this is what God has been leading up to all along."

Dad began to research abortion and post-abortion syndrome in depth. He interviewed women who suffered as Cindy and I had, and we anticipated the day God would allow us to stand as a family and tell our story.

By the time I spoke at the Real Choices luncheon, we knew God's plan didn't include Dad speaking out publicly about abortion. Dad's fall down the stairs in March of 2007 had made his recall of the newest things he had learned nonexistent. But I invited him to the podium when I concluded my talk, and the words he spoke I will cling to all of my days.

Choking back his tears, Daddy put his arm around me, leaned into the microphone, and said, "It's very hard, Little One. But I'm so proud of you, that you were willing to do what you just did. And I believe your message will impact a lot of people. We do have a God who forgives us, because He understands us, He created us. I'm proud of my Little One—that's what I always call her, Little One, my youngest daughter."

Then Dad looked straight at me and said, "I've never been as proud of you, and I've always been proud of you, but I've never been as proud as I am at this moment, Little One. Because as you know, my life has been committed to helping other people, and I believe right now that you made some statements that will impact the lives of many people right in this room, and they will impact others. I'm just grateful that God entrusted you to us, and I'm grateful that you are the editor of my books."

Even my earthly father is still glad I am his. After all I have done, my daddy is still glad God gave me to him and to Mom. And he is proud of me. After so many years of living with my shame, Dad's words of encouragement were a blessing beyond measure.

FORGIVENESS

My first true experience of forgiving someone for something extremely hurtful happened when I was eleven years old. Remember my adorable pet chipmunk named Chicker? Well, she had a cage that she ate in and sometimes slept in, but I left the door to the cage open so she could run and play all over the house. I awoke every morning to find her sitting upright on my pillow, paws held tentatively in front of her, studying my face. I tried not to move so she would stay close, but the moment she saw my eyes flutter she'd dart off the bed and into hiding.

Every summer our family went to Mississippi to visit both of my grandmothers, and Mom would hire someone to take care of the dogs, cats, and any other animals we happened to have. Mom always insisted that Chicker be in her cage when we left town, so she wouldn't scare the pet-sitter with one of her sudden and unexpected appearances.

Even inside, catching Chicker was a feat, and the morning before we were due to leave on our trip Mom saw that Chicker had climbed up on the inside of the screen in her open bedroom window and was taking in the sights and sounds of the great outdoors. Mom knew if she could close the window fast enough, Chicker would be trapped, so she rushed to shut the window. Just as it slammed down, Chicker jumped to make her escape.

When I awoke that morning, I saw my mother, arms extended towards me, tears streaming down her face, and my precious chipmunk lying lifeless across her upturned palms. My mother's grief was so great, so intense, so complete. "I'm sorry, I'm so sorry," she whispered. "I killed Chicker." Through her tears Mom told me what had happened.

Never had I seen my mother so distressed. Her remorse was consuming her, and I couldn't bear it that she felt so desperately sad. I jumped out of bed and hugged her, repeating over and over, "It's okay, Mama. It's okay. You didn't know she would jump."

For the first time in my life, my concern was not for myself. I accepted my mother's apology; her remorse told me how utterly and completely she regretted what had happened. The compassion I felt for her welled up instantaneously, my forgiveness was total, and though I mourned for my chipmunk, my concern for my mother was far greater.

Can you imagine how much more compassion our heavenly Father has for us when we come to Him, broken and grieved, extending before Him, honestly and openly, the very thing we did that we know has broken His heart?

Often the things that grieve us most are buried deep in an attempt to escape the pain, but what we will not admit cannot be dealt with—or forgiven.

I believe that even though we might have quit a behavior, when we pretend the offending behavior never existed and fail to deal with the reality of the consequences of our actions, we put ourselves in the position God warned me about—the position of "un-use-ability," where the underlying guilt makes us feel unworthy to be used by God for the benefit of others.

It concerns me deeply that our churches are full of people who "believe" in Jesus, yet many, many of those professing to know Him have never read His Word for themselves. They don't even know if the way they are living, or if the choices they are making, are pleasing to God or an abomination, because they don't know what God has said about how we, as Christians, are to live.

Many have never repented, much less admitted that their sins needed to be forgiven by God. They haven't experienced the pain of having broken His heart because, while they believe that Jesus exists, they have not surrendered their lives to Him and made Him Lord.

I meet women and men who walked the aisles of the church and got baptized without believing—like I did—and though they still go to church, they are hurting and lost. I want so badly for them to know the love and the truth, the power and the freedom of a one-on-one, intimate relationship with the living God.

My coming to trust and know Jesus was a long, long process. I do believe I was saved at that Bill Gothard Basic Youth Conflicts seminar when I was sixteen because of the way sin grieved my heart from then on. I tried to improve my behavior and choices as I grew older, but I believed I had fallen from God's grace, so I never drew on His power. I did everything I did in my own power and always, always failed.

It wasn't until my husband and I separated that I knew for sure that I had grown enough in my faith that I wanted what

God wanted more than what I wanted. From that point on, my growth has been steady. My understanding of God's Word and how I am to live as one of His deepens continually as I read and study the Bible. Life, even the hardest parts, becomes easier every day because of my intimate relationship with Christ.

COLUMBUS, OHIO, NOVEMBER 13, 2007

I can't recall which hotel we were staying in when it happened, but I was on my knees praying for the people who would hear me interview Dad at the Get Motivated Seminar later that day. My prayer was suddenly infused with the need to surrender my life completely to Jesus. I knew and believed I was already His, but I had never said to Him, "Lord, my life is none of my business. My life is Yours. Here I am, send me. Where You want me to go, I will go."

Yes, I was as available, willing, and obedient as I could be and I felt I was doing as He would have me do, so the submission was a little confusing. I am thankful I have learned not to question God and put things off (most of the time), so I did as I was impressed to do. I said, "YES, FATHER—I will go where You want me to go. I will do what You want me to do. My life is none of my business."

Lightning didn't strike. Lights didn't flash, and angels didn't suddenly appear. Instead, the most amazing peace came over me and, praise God, ALL of my FEAR OF THE FUTURE fell away! True liberty was mine! I had no idea my anxiety about the future was related to believing I could hold on to and continue to control the parts of my life I hadn't placed in God's hands. I've let Jesus direct my path and trusted Him completely with the direction it has taken me since that day (except for one quick trip to the cabin for some "are you sure about this, God?" questions). I am on a journey that amazes me, and I can't wait to see what's next!

The Little Mouse

One afternoon I was standing in the kitchen when our cat Rosedale burst through the cat door with a mouse in her mouth. It was very much alive, and in short order it got away from her. Suddenly, the mouse was running in my direction with Rosedale in hot pursuit—you should know that I have had pet mice and pet rats all my life, so I am not in the least afraid of them!

I started yelling, "Come to me, little mouse, I will save you! Come to me, I will save you!" And the little mouse ran right into my feet. As I reached down to scoop it up, it took one look at me with eyes as big as saucers and ran back in the direction it had come from, disappearing around the corner of the breakfast bar.

That mouse chose to go back to an almost certain death rather than trust me. The mouse was at least familiar with cats, deadly though they were. I was so big and so powerful by comparison—but mostly the little mouse just didn't know who I was or if it could really trust me.

A few moments later the mouse was running toward me again. Rosedale was swatting at it with both paws, knocking it off course, this way and that. I was once again yelling, "Come to me, little mouse, I will save you, I will save you—come to me!" With death breathing down its neck, the little mouse made it back to my feet and allowed me to scoop it out of harm's way. I cupped the terrified mouse to my chest, and it pressed its tiny forehead hard against me. Rosedale sat at my feet, ears half-flattened, looking up with angry eyes, her tail twitching hard in disgust at the turn of events.

What are you running from? More important, what and who are you running to? Have you heard someone calling your name... "Come to Me, I will save you. Come to Me, I will save you"? They are open wide—run into the arms of Jesus. He will save you.

CHAPTER THIRTEEN

GROW UP AND BE YOUR BEST

WARNING—DO NOT ENTER

God Himself wants us to be the best person we can be, and He continually moves to shape and mold us into becoming the "right kind" of person. When Dad turned his life over to Jesus on July 4, 1972, God had soft, easy-to-mold clay to work with. When God got hold of me...well, let's just say I'd been left out to bake awhile. I was somewhat hardened into some bad thinking patterns that needed lots of work!

Have you ever been on a road trip and driven through a small town that has seen better times? It's kind of sad. Empty, decaying, dilapidated buildings are a testament to the thriving commerce that once existed there, but all that is left are empty shells that look as though they are about to collapse in on themselves. Oftentimes you'll see the familiar yellow and black warning tape strung around the perimeter of each building. In huge, bold, block letters you can read the words one after another: DO NOT ENTER—WARNING— DO NOT ENTER—WARNING—DO NOT ENTER.

I wish our minds had DO NOT ENTER warning tape that would automatically throw itself up when we try to barge recklessly back into thoughts of pain and misery from our past. If we allow our minds to dwell on the past, it is a sure sign we have yet to go all the way THROUGH the past and have a ways to go before we can get BEYOND the past.

My dad says that after God, the most important person you'll talk to all day is yourself! I know that to be a fact. Has your mind ever started a conversation with you? Has it said stuff like, *"Who do YOU think you are? You can't do THAT! You've NEVER done anything like THAT before. What makes YOU think you can do something THAT big? You don't have what it takes...remember that last deal you tried to convince me you could do? How'd that work for ya? I told you then and I'm telling you now...you're NOT smart enough, you don't have the skill set, and besides, NOBODY believes you can do ANYTHING right. Honestly, why even try?"*

Friend, if your mind talks to you with that tone and spews harsh, hurtful untruths like that—YOU are the only one who can stop it! You have to set the boundaries. You have to boot that kind of self-talk out of your mind and out of your life.

There is an old saying that goes, "Your mind is like a bad neighborhood, you should never visit there alone!" Because of my faith, I ask God to accompany me when I get into what Dad calls "stinkin' thinkin'." I have learned through the years that replacing detrimental thoughts with inspiring ones is imperative to growth and to keeping the enemy from getting the upper hand. If you don't happen to be a spiritual person, you might consider that you could, on occasion, be your own worst enemy. If you are a spiritual person, you might want to consider that sometimes Satan doesn't need any help with dragging you down—you do a good enough job all by yourself!

You have to DECIDE to be THROUGH with your past and then you have to take your thoughts captive, a skill I learned from Scripture that really works!

When I finally learned how to take captive the thoughts I didn't want to have, I was able to quit smoking. This is how it works: When the impulse to have a cigarette presented itself to my mind, my thoughts said, *Have a cigarette...you want a cigarette...you neeeed a cigarette.* Then my mind would show me a mental picture of myself enjoying a cigarette. My mind would say *Look...see how much more relaxed you'll feel? Now, won't that be so much better? One won't hurt. Go ahead...you'll feel soooooo much better!*

That's how my quitting smoking self-talk would go every time. Fortunately, I learned from previous efforts to quit smoking that the serious craving only lasted about three minutes, so I knew I only had to hold the thought at bay for three minutes.

For three minutes, every time the thought of having a cigarette pushed itself into my mind, I immediately ushered it out with a yellow and black WARNING—DO NOT ENTER tape of my own. Over and over I would repeat to myself, *Don't entertain the thought. Don't entertain the thought.*

That meant that I would not allow myself to "see" myself having a cigarette. I would not allow myself to think about how much I wanted one or how it would taste or how I would feel if I had one. I just would not allow my mind to consider smoking.

Obviously, it took some practice, but I was willing to do it poorly until I could learn to do it well. I didn't give up trying just because I failed the first twenty or thirty times. I kept it up until I mastered it. I did not allow my mind to tell me what I could or couldn't do. I told my mind what I would do, and then I did it... and I started over until I got it right. Taking thoughts captive and escorting them out of your mind takes practice, but it gets easier with each success.

When thoughts of the past enter your mind, don't entertain them—escort them out.

Becoming your BEST you starts with self-examination...a truth session...a hard look at reality. What are the facts of your life? Do you have trouble getting along with others? Is there a long list of people you have resentment toward or who have resentment toward you? Do you always get your way, even if you have to be pushy about it, or are you the type that people run over and take advantage of? Do you catch heat for not following through on your commitments? Or do you get teased and criticized for being a perfectionist who is never finished with a project? Do you wonder why life seems harder for you than it appears to be for other people?

If you related to these questions, quit worrying about them right now. Every one of those situations will be a thing of your past if you can answer the next question in the affirmative: Are you ready for a fulfilling, exciting challenge that will position you to make a positive difference in your own life and in the lives of others? If you are, you are ready to become what my father calls "the right kind of person."

YOU'LL KNOW WHEN YOU ARE READY!

I was ready to start seriously and persistently becoming the right kind of person when I got sick and tired of my actions—or inaction—and I knew I was powerless to change anything on my own. Every day for me was full of fear and discontentment because of something I had left undone, a discussion I didn't want to have, or a conflict I had (either real or blown out of proportion in my mind) with my husband or children.

I was an acceptance seeker and a people pleaser. I lived my life in accordance with what I thought others expected of me. I did whatever I thought I had to do to be accepted, and I became addicted to the positive reinforcement I got when I did anything thoughtful or above and beyond what was expected.

If you didn't look pleased with me, I started coming apart from the inside out. I was too afraid to ask you if I had let you down or not lived up to your expectations. To me, your approval meant I must be the "right kind" of person—that I was okay. If you weren't happy with me, in my mind I was on the brink of losing your love, friendship, respect, or all of the above. Since I wasn't depending on God as my source of strength and approval, losing your good favor meant I was totally alone.

Sometimes the stress of having to do something I'd never done before drove me to eat compulsively, or to stay in bed too long, or to reach for another drink. Different people use different things to avoid dealing with issues that need work. Some people use working long hours as an escape, or in the name of relaxing or for their health, adopt hobbies or exercise routines that take up almost all of their free time.

Others volunteer to the point their own family is neglected. If you're doing something you believe you need to do, or helping out someone else, that can't be bad, can it? If you're trying to get ahead in life and have to work long hours and every weekend, that can't be bad, can it?

I love what author/speaker Denise Taylor says about how she dealt with her daughter Jonnae's leukemia in her book, *Heavenly Birth: A Mother's Journey—A Daughter's Legacy*. She said, "I know I'm doing a good job, given the circumstances, maybe even a great job, but I also know I AM capable of better. It's what we know in our heart that gives us peace. How everyone else views our progress or performance isn't a measure of contentment."

Denise Taylor is right: only you know your heart. If you struggle with any of these problems, I hope to inspire you to want to make the positive changes that will make a positive difference in your life and the lives of those you love. If you are like Denise Taylor, and in the eyes of others you appear to be doing exceptionally well but you know in your heart you can do better, I hope you will take up my challenge of DECIDING to be

THROUGH with your past, getting help if you need it, and moving on to become the right kind of person!

What Is the "Right Kind" of Person?

Being the right kind of person means that you are compassionate toward others, you are rigorously honest, consistent, dependable, trustworthy, sincere, approachable, humble, kind, and loving. You love the opportunity to help others in need, and you share what you have without strings attached. The Good Samaritan was the right kind of person.

The right kind of person is concerned about the welfare of others and considers the opportunity to help a blessing, not an inconvenience. Most everyone can recall an occasion when a total stranger went out of their way to help. I know of at least three different occasions when someone helped my father with his wardrobe. If you travel as many hundreds of thousands of miles as my father has, it's just a matter of time until you've forgotten an important article of clothing. My father has had people give him the tie off their neck, their cufflinks, and he once had to borrow a belt.

One of my fellow speakers on the Get Motivated platform had to borrow a pair of shoes, and I saw one of our speakers with his suit coat on and no shirt...he had taken it off and given it to a fellow speaker who had forgotten to pack his white shirt.

Maybe you've had someone rescue you when you ran out of gas or you had a flat tire. Or possibly someone rescued you when you least expected it. My daughter DeDe's husband, Gus, who is now cured of cancer, was having one of his many chemo treatments in the hospital. DeDe decided to go downstairs to get a bite to eat and was waiting for the elevator to arrive on her floor. The elevator doors opened to reveal a lone, weeping woman inside.

When you spend a lot of time on an oncology floor, you understand this scenario; tears happen. My beautiful daughter took one look, stepped back, tilted her head to the side, and motioned the woman off the elevator and into her open arms. She held her close and never said a word. When the serious tears were past, the woman lifted her head off my daughter's shoulder, and a look passed between them that only those who have shared the same battle can understand. Without a word, the woman went on her way, and DeDe waited for the next elevator.

A few nurses had been watching the unexpected exchange and asked DeDe if she knew the woman. DeDe said she did not. They told her they had never seen such a compassionate act. DeDe did not know the woman, but she knew her pain and was there to comfort her. That is a wonderful example of being the right kind of person—a person who is concerned for the welfare of others...even total strangers.

The right kind of person sincerely wants to do what is right and what is fair. They will often relinquish what is rightfully theirs in the interest of saving a relationship, because relationships are more important to them than things.

One of the main reasons my husband and I love living in

Alvord, Texas, is the wonderful people. When our neighbors Shelba and Vernon Ruddick decided to put up a fence between our place and theirs, we noticed that they staked the fence line well inside of their property line. The stakes from the survey that had been done when we bought our property were still visible, and we pointed out to Vernon that he was at least a few feet too far on his side. Vernon said he'd far rather give up a few feet of land than take a chance on having any kind of misunderstanding with a good neighbor. The Ruddicks are a perfect example of valuing people and relationships over things.

Amazingly, we had a similar occurrence with our neighbors on the opposite side of our property when our legal survey didn't match what they had always believed to be true about their property line. Instead of any hard feelings, they just said everything was fine and if they ever sold their place we'd all know more when the new survey was done.

Seeing and experiencing the natural generosity of people like my neighbors makes those of us who are not yet generous feel ashamed at how tightly we hold on to our stuff. Generous folks like that will offer to spring for the meal ticket and are genuinely happy to get to treat you. Imagine your amazement when the beautiful vase you admired at a friend's home last week shows up on your doorstep, via UPS with a little note saying, "I saw how your eyes lit up when you admired this vase. I want you to have and enjoy it!" Being in the company of the right kind of person blesses you in several ways—one of them is that it helps highlight your own areas of growth if you are actively seeking to be your best you.

The right kind of person knows that life is about loving and forgiving and being there when you're needed. Sometimes it's easier to give an example of the opposite kind of behavior, as in the illustration below, in order to make a point. Have you ever gotten upset with someone and just let them have a big, overly loud piece of your mind and later discovered that your assumption about what had happened had been completely off base and that your behavior was anything but loving?

THE JUMPING JACK RUSSELL

One day I was driving to visit my parents, and I was about to cross one of the bridges over the highway bypass in our tiny town when I saw a little orange and white Jack Russell terrier trot onto the bridge.

I slowed my car down to give the dog plenty of time and space to get across the fairly narrow two-lane bridge when suddenly an eighteen-wheeler turned onto the bridge behind the little dog. That dog took one look over her shoulder, trotted over to the solid concrete wall that ran the length of either side of the bridge, and hopped right over it!

I gasped. I knew the dog had fallen at least eighteen feet to the freeway below, and I was afraid that the dog had fallen into oncoming traffic. I swung my car over to the side of the service road, slammed it into PARK, jumped out, and ran down the embankment.

Luckily, the dog had fallen onto the shoulder of the road and wasn't in danger of being hit, but she was lying on her side, shaking. When I got close to her, she tried to stand up, and it became obvious that she had hurt one of her front legs. She allowed me to pick her up, and I was relieved to find that she had a dog tag with the name Rosie on it and what appeared to be her owner's phone number.

I got back in my car, put the little dog in the passenger seat, dug out my reading glasses, and immediately called the number. A lady answered. My adrenaline was still pumping from all the drama and I said with great urgency, "You don't know me. I have your dog Rosie. She's hurt. She just jumped off the highway bridge and landed on the shoulder about twenty feet below. Can I bring her to you?"

Silence.

"What do you want me to do with your dog?" I asked.

She said, "That's not my dog."

Confused, I replied, "Why does she have your phone number on her tag?"

Somewhat exasperated, she said, "She used to be my dog."

Once again I asked, "What do you want me to do with her? She's hurt and needs medical attention."

With great disdain, she said, "I don't know what to tell you to do. I can't deal with that dog!"

The shock and horror of someone blowing off such a cute, sweet, and suffering little dog that they had once owned hit me full force. With all the self-righteous indignation I could muster up, I angrily said, "You obviously don't deserve to own a dog!" And I hung up the phone.

I rushed the little dog to my vet, told her to give her anything she needed, and said I'd stop back in on my way home and decide what to do then.

My self-righteous self wasn't back in my car five minutes until it started—that little voice that often sounds mysteriously like my dad's: *Julie, you don't know that woman. You have no idea what she might be going through. Who are you to treat anyone that way? You'd better call her back...you'd better call her and apologize. Julie...*

I resisted long enough to drive the hour to my folks' house, have lunch with them, and visit for a while, but as soon as I was alone in my car that little voice started back up again, and I knew it was useless to resist. If I was going to have to apologize, I might as well get it over with. I pulled over and dialed the woman's number. When she answered I said in a rush, "Please don't hang up. I'm the lady who called you about the dog, and I need to tell you how sorry I am that I spoke to you the way I did. I don't know you or what might be going on in your life, and I have no right to judge you or treat you badly. Can you forgive me?"

She said, "I'm so glad you called back. I've been thinking all day what a jerk you must think I am. When you called I had a car full of little boys who'd had a sleepover at my house last night. We were on the way to the hospital because my son was born with a chronic disease that requires immediate treatment when it flares up, and he was having another episode. I just couldn't think of what I could do at that moment for Rosie."

She went on to explain that her family lived in an area that had lots of traffic and major busy streets and that Rosie was an escape artist. They had given her to the no-kill animal shelter with instructions to only give her to a family who lived in the country because they were sure she'd get run over if she continued to live in the city. They had done all they could to keep her in, but they simply couldn't keep her safe.

Ultimately, the little dog's broken foot healed just fine, and we found the family who had adopted her. What if I hadn't already accepted the challenge to live a more godly life and become the right kind of person? I hate to think of the added burden I would have left on that poor mother's shoulders, had I not called her back to apologize.

I Want to Be the "Right Kind" of Person

The right kind of person is selfless but also knows how to set healthy boundaries for others who may not yet be the right kind of person.

The right kind of person is who I want to be, regardless of my circumstances. Being the right kind of person holds a place of importance in my life today that I didn't even know existed twenty years ago. My transparency and authenticity rest 100 percent on my willingness to hold myself accountable to God for being the right kind of person. Without Him and His provision, strength, and power, being the right kind of person would still be beyond my ability and my grasp.

CHAPTER FOURTEEN

ATTITUDE AND CHOICES

YOU GET TO CHOOSE

No book titled *Growing Up Ziglar* would be complete without at least some in-depth discussion about attitude. Some people actually believe that choosing to have a positive attitude is the same as choosing to be phony. They believe that a positive attitude glosses over reality, and that it is simply an act and a way to stay in denial about the harsh reality of life. However, the attitude you do choose, whether it be positive or negative, is the attitude that shades your perspective on life and how you'll live it each day. In fact, not choosing your attitude is a choice that will keep you on an emotional roller coaster.

The characteristics of the right kind of person lend themselves to a positive, can-do attitude. A defeatist, negative attitude can be a reflection of a "what's in it for me," self-centered person or even a jealous person. We all know individuals who make it their business to be against whatever we are for. If you tell them you're buying a particular car, they'll tell you all of the problems with that car. It doesn't matter what you're doing, where you're going, or even what you choose to eat for dinner, they'll find something wrong with it. You know who they are...she's the friend you won't give your plumber's number to, or your electrician's, or your carpet cleaner's because it doesn't matter how good a job they do, your friend will find something to complain about, and they'll blame it on you for recommending them! Nobody enjoys being around people like that!

When I talk about what it was like growing up with Mr. Positive Attitude himself, I enjoy teasing about waking up to an "opportunity clock" instead of an alarm clock. I point out that most families look forward to the weekend; not the Ziglar family, we looked forward to the "strong end." When we got the sniffles we had a "warm," not a cold.

I also explain that Dad has always practiced what he preaches. Dad believes that you have to put good stuff into your mind to get good stuff out of your mind. To that end, I'd occasionally wake up to hear my father whispering near my ear, "Little One, you're going to have a fantastic day today. All your friends are going to be so happy to see you. You're going to make straight As and your attitude is going to be cheerful and positive." I'm blessed that Dad put in the effort to help me be the best I can be.

The fact is, after Dad became a Christian, he never had to worry because he knew God had everything under control. When you have no concerns about the future, and your past is already taken care of, a positive attitude is the natural result. When Dad learned that his memory loss was permanent and getting worse, his comment to me was, "You know, Little One, it's kind of sad to think of all of this [his speaking career] coming to an end, but when I consider what lies ahead of me, I can't help but be excited. Jesus said He was going ahead of me to prepare a place so wonderful, so magnificent, that the mind cannot fathom its grandeur. I'm really looking forward to that."

I believe that is Dad's secret to being happy and positive. He is ALWAYS looking forward to the next great and wonderful thing. He is aware and certain of what lies ahead of him.

My dad has long held that a positive attitude won't make it possible for you to do anything, but it will make it possible for you to do everything *better* than a negative attitude will. Some people mistakenly credit my dad with saying, "If you think it, you can achieve it," or "If you believe it, you can achieve it." Those two statements simply are not true, and my dad never said either one of them.

There is a difference between positive thinking and unrealistic expectations. If you've watched *American Idol*, you've seen person after person who thought and BELIEVED they were a great singer get told no. Some of them protest and say all their friends tell them how great they are, but it doesn't change the reality that they are horrible singers. They thought they were great, they believed they were great, but no matter how much they believed it, they didn't achieve it. The concept of "If you believe it, you can achieve it" has given positive thinking a bad name.

Consider this situation: When I was a teenager, showing my horse was my passion. We finally got good enough that I decided to take my mare to an A-level show in the big coliseum at Dallas Fair Park where the best of the best went. To my shock and disappointment—and the disappointment of my father—I discovered my hunter would not jump indoors. The large majority of A-level shows are indoors. Dad encouraged me to sell my horse and said he'd help me buy another one.

It was hard, but I parted with my mare and put the 350 dollars aside for when I found my dream horse. It took almost a year of serious horse shopping, but I found the horse I wanted, and the price tag was one thousand dollars, a lot of money back in 1971. With great excitement I told Dad I'd need 650 dollars to buy the horse I'd found.

He got this crestfallen look on his face and told me he'd just sunk all his extra money into self-publishing his first book and he couldn't help me right then. I wanted that horse so much I completely skipped having a bad attitude about Dad not being able to help, and I went for the CAN-DO attitude instead. I'd find a way to get that horse. I called the owners and asked if I could put 350 dollars down and pay out the rest over time. They agreed! And I got the horse I'd set my heart on.

I had to choose not to be upset with Dad. I had to choose not to let Dad's circumstances kill my dream. I had to choose not to be a victim. I had to choose to be responsible for my own dream and do what I could to make it happen. I had to choose the can-do attitude. Without it, I would not have tried to get the horse.

I had been free to respond either way. I was FREE to choose my attitude then and I am still free to choose my attitude now. Nobody and no circumstance can take that freedom away from me—or you!

Here's why that is important: We are all free to choose our attitude toward what others think about us, and we can even choose our attitude toward what we perceive others think about us. We are free to NOT CARE what others think, real or imagined! The only thing that matters is what we know to be true about ourselves. If we are people of faith, we'll care what God thinks of us, but man's opinion will not be a concern. Now that will SET YOU FREE! I will remember forever the day I knew I had nothing to hide and nothing to fear. That was the day I let go of what others thought and concentrated on pleasing God and being the best me one day at a time.

If I had understood that attitude when we moved to Texas, I would not have fallen into bad choices like I did. I would have stood tall, and over time my good reputation would have proven itself. Oh, the things people do based on what we think others think.

BAD ATTITUDE REGRET

If there is one attitude I could go back and change in my life it would be the negative attitude I had toward my incredible body. I spent so much time loathing what I perceived were my imperfections that I never appreciated the miracle of what my body did for me and how the peculiar little things about it helped make me uniquely me. How many hours did I spend wishing I looked different when, in fact, in hindsight, I can see that I looked just fine, or as my dad would say, even better than good? Countless, countless wasted hours I spent wallowing in self-induced dissatisfaction.

In no other area of my life have I wasted so much time fretting about what was really fine. In no other area of my life did I compare myself so often and so critically to so many. I can remember peeking out from under my sunglasses when I was lying on the beach. I was slim and trim and in my early twenties, and I was watching the older women talk and walk as the incoming waves lapped at their feet. Even then, I recognized that they had a freedom that was foreign to me. Even then I thought that I couldn't wait until I was old enough to not care what other people thought of my body so that I, too, could truly enjoy a casual walk on the beach with friends. Somehow I knew the day would come when cellulite, varicose veins, wrinkles, and even fat rolls, if I had some, wouldn't ruin my day. Oh, how I wish I'd allowed that attitude of total acceptance to come earlier. There is no room for an attitude of self-consciousness in a life that is all it can be.

Accepting what you can't change, changing what you can, and knowing how to discern the difference is absolutely the most important step in choosing an attitude that will allow you to be 100 percent content all the time. Trusting God with ALL of your life makes it possible.

Change Makes for Choices

Choice making is critical to success, and change is the one element that forces more choices to be made than any other. It doesn't matter if it is a gradual change, like growing older, or a planned change, like making a move to a larger home to accommodate your growing family, or a sudden, unexpected change, like our family experienced when my father fell down the stairs and suffered a brain injury. All change challenges the process of choice making and can even, at times, make people question God.

Most people seem to resist change. Some even admit to hating change, and their inability to "go with the flow" throws them into a tizzy that can result in a meltdown of major proportions. I know people who refuse to acknowledge that changes have even occurred. They stay in denial about their circumstances and avoid making any new choices based on the changes. Unfortunately, that attitude escalates and complicates their problems.

The main reason change, especially unexpected change, gets a bad rap and throws people for such a loop is because of fear that the change will take something from us we either want or need. With change comes choice making, and anyone who has lived very long knows that the choices we make determine the results we get.

When my dad fell down the staircase in his home in March of 2007, I learned a very important lesson—when the tidal wave of change comes, don't fight the current! Start looking for a surf-board! Riding the crest of change with enthusiasm will get you so much further in life than treading the water of what is, what was, or what might have been.

If you suddenly find that your circumstances have changed, you either choose to change with them or sink! When Dad suffered his head injury and the profound short-term memory loss that followed, we were faced with literally hundreds of choices that needed to be made quickly. Dad's whole focus was on how he could keep encouraging and helping people in a new way that would accommodate the changes that had taken place.

He never considered that his career was finished; he only considered how he could continue forward with an even bigger purpose. His choice to see the new opportunity, instead of the end of life as he knew it, is exactly what anyone who knows Zig Ziglar would expect from him.

Dad had decided what kind of choices he would make long before he fell down the stairs. He had become the right kind of person and developed the character traits that allowed him to make his choices based on principles and faith, rather than emotions such as fear, anger, doubt, or a feeling of defeat.

Dad knew the purpose of his life was encouraging others, and he saw the problems brought on by the fall as a temporary setback. His background in sales had taught him that obstacles could be overcome by discovering the felt need of your customer. Dad simply treated himself as his own customer and employed what he already knew to find creative ways to continue on. He just needed more options to continue what he had decided to do in advance. We can be ready for change and the unforeseen by making our choices in advance.

When I was a straight-commission salesperson, I discovered that the biggest challenge I had was readjusting my attitude after every change in territory and every change in commission structure. Each time my territory changed, it meant I lost existing customers, and I would have to spend lots of time learning who my prospects were in the new territory, not to mention the time I spent trying to find out if they'd been called on by anyone in my company in the past.

I'd get hot under the collar, fuss, and fume and be upset that I had to start all over. I didn't like change, especially change that, in my opinion, undermined my ability to make a living. Then about the time I'd get used to the new territory, I'd find out our commission structure had changed and it was going to be a lot harder to make the kind of money I was used to making. Every change the executives made impacted my bottom line, and my demeanor. I became suspicious...and I lived in a state of "what's next?" I was as miserable as I could be, until I realized how my attitude was hurting my sales. I was spending more time fuming than I was dialing the phone. My bottom line suffered because I wasn't selling, not because I had a new territory or a new commission structure. When I decided in advance that I would not let future changes throw me off track, and that I would immediately accept the changes as facts, not personal attacks, I was not only happier, I made more money.

Our choices do determine our circumstances. We can't always know in advance how some of our choices will impact us or the ones we love, but we can trace our present circumstances back to a choice we made or a choice we failed to make. Invariably, the choices we make based purely on emotion are the ones we are most likely to regret. I mention this again because if you are not yet the "right kind" of person, you're still on track to make future choices that will end up in your "hindsight" hall of fame.

STANLEY

One of my most memorable "hindsight" stories is related to a choice based 100 percent on fear. If you have never had a naked man knock on your front door, or had your horse commandeered by the sheriff so he could hunt for car thieves that might be hiding in your cattle feeders, you may need some help understanding how I ended up with a vicious St. Bernard named Stanley Alouishis.

The day the naked man knocked on the front door, I happened to look out of the kitchen window just in time to see our dogs running around the side of the house, tails waggin'. I stepped outside and went to see what they were so excited about, and just as I cleared the corner of the house, I saw a naked man knocking on my front door!

I ran back inside and told my husband there was a naked man knocking on the front door. Because we live in Texas and we can, he grabbed his shotgun, told me to stay put, and rushed outside to confront our visitor. Moments later I heard him yell, "Grab that tree and spread 'em!"

About five minutes later, my husband yelled for me to get some clothes for the man. Turns out the poor fellow had been kidnapped and robbed, and the thieves took everything he had, including his clothes! They dumped him out on the little one-lane dirt road behind our property.

Just over a week later, I was riding one of our horses on our back forty acres when a sheriff came barreling down that same little one-lane dirt road where the naked man had been dumped. When he saw me, he slammed on his brakes, threw the car into PARK, jumped out, and left his door wide open. He climbed through the barbed wire fence and yelled across the field, "I'm commandeering your horse! I think there might be car thieves hiding in your cattle feeders."

I rode over to him, jumped down, and held the horse while he mounted, and away he went! There I was, standing all alone in the pasture, looking at the running squad car and thinking to myself, *If I were a car thief I'd kidnap me and take off in that squad car.*

The sheriff was back in about ten minutes and said he and his deputies would like to check out our barn and outbuildings and asked me to ride back up to my house and meet them there.

I was standing in the driveway when they arrived, and all three of my dogs stood there with me, tails a-waggin', so happy to see the latest strangers arrive. They even got in on the act of helping look for the car thieves. For all I knew, the dogs had shown them where to hide! The whole situation was upsetting.

My husband and I lived so far out in the country, you had to head toward town to go hunting. It took an hour to drive to the grocery store, and our closest neighbor was almost two miles away. Suddenly, I did not feel safe when my husband left for work...and, silly me, I had always thought the country was so much safer than the city!

That's when I made a decision based on the emotion of fear and the pressure of the immediate (a really bad combination). I decided I needed a mean dog...a real watchdog...a dog that could protect me. We found Stanley on death row. He was a "three times and you're out" dog. He had bitten three people, so we knew he was the dog we wanted. The pound allowed us to sign papers saying we knew he was a vicious dog and that we accepted responsibility for him.

You should have seen the slobber sling from that dog's mouth when he was trying to bite my husband. We couldn't even get him out of the pickup truck when we got home from the pound! My husband had to park the truck in the shade, and while I distracted Stanley, he'd rush in and put food and water in the bed of the truck. It took three days for the dog to allow my husband to untie the rope and get him out of the truck. Stanley turned out to be so good at his job that we had to keep him tied up—so he wouldn't bite me!

One day when my husband was at work I happened to look out the window just as Stanley broke his rope. He rushed over to the horse paddock where he began chasing a yearling colt we had on consignment. I knew that even if Stanley didn't catch and maul the colt, he was going to drive him through the fence. Without another thought, I took off after Stanley.

I finally got a good hold on the rope he was dragging, and he proceeded to pull me around that paddock like a water skier behind a motorboat. With each lurch forward, Stanley was gaining on the colt. Suddenly, Stanley stopped, and it dawned on me all too quickly that I had a serious problem.

A hundred and fifty pounds of the meanest dog I'd ever seen was facing me down at the end of a rope I didn't dare let go of. I had to make my move. It was me or him. With everything I had, I started yelling, "Bad dog! Bad dog!" Boldness came out of the depths of my fear and I got as big and tall as I could and started taking big strides toward him, reeling him in with big yanks and jerks. "Bad dog! Bad dog!" As I pulled him closer, I could see his eyes starting to avert in an act of submission. By the time I had him in front of me, he had turned onto his back—and from that moment on that dog was MY DOG!

The ability to make wise choices sometimes comes with learning the hard way—by experiencing the consequences of bad choices and developing an honest desire to avoid those consequences at all costs. When you get honest with yourself, admit you made a bad choice in the emotion and fear of the moment, and take responsibility for your choices, then you can begin to right your wrongs and redirect your path.

Regardless of how you come to the place of being the right kind of person, true success in life comes when the choices you make during times of change are wisdom-based, not fear-based, and grounded in a desire to please God.

CHAPTER FIFTEEN

THE NEXT RIGHT THING

INTEGRITY CHECK

When you know *Whose* you are, what you stand for, and why you stand for it, you know how to "BE" who you are. When you are the right kind of person with the character traits we have already covered, you get to enjoy the true advantage of having God-given power and the ability to make the best possible choices.

Earlier I said you have to BE before you can DO. If you are not honest, if you don't have good values and motives, you won't be the kind of person who will DO the next right thing because you will make choices based on bad reasoning. But, the right kind of person naturally gravitates toward good choices for themselves and for the benefit of others.

Twenty-five years ago when I first started working on becoming the right kind of person, I was asked to be rigorously honest. I thought I was honest and said as much. Then I was given a challenge, the same challenge I am giving you now: Begin today carrying an index card and pencil. For the next three days, every time you say anything that is not absolutely accurate or truthful, grab your pencil and give yourself an X. I recommend you even take notes on how you bent the truth.

Give yourself an X for "excuses" that aren't entirely true. For instance, if you procrastinated about getting ready and made yourself late for an appointment, but you said, "I'm sorry I'm late, the traffic was horrible!" that deserves an X. Give yourself an X for exaggerations like, "I held a meeting last night and there were easily seventy-five people there," when, realistically, it would be pushing it to say there were fifty in attendance.

Maybe you deserve an X because you walked into the house thirty minutes later than you said you would arrive and announced that a coworker held you up, but actually you decided to have a Starbucks with a friend on the way home and just didn't want to be honest with your spouse.

Or, have you ever announced on a Saturday morning that you have to be gone all day and you're sorry you forgot to mention it earlier, when in reality it hadn't slipped your mind at all—you just dreaded seeing the disappointment on the face of your loved one, so you put it off?

Do you ever try to make a good story better by embellishing the facts? Give yourself an X for every single time you exaggerate, for every single time you tell a white lie or you lie by omission, or you just outright lie. If you're already the right kind of person, you probably won't have an X for your three-day period. If you are the kind of person who is used to justifying your behavior and trying to fly under the radar, you will probably have a card full of Xs and proof that there is room for improvement. As long as there is room for improvement in this area, you are going to live a life that is convoluted, complicated, stressful, and so much less than it can be.

If you discover that you have a long way to go before you become your best you, don't get discouraged. You can break this sad habit of not being rigorously honest—even if you have to embarrass yourself and say, "Let me set that straight—it was fifty, not seventy-five like I initially said." Then quickly apologize to Father God for your slip. Do that to yourself often enough and you'll leave the lie off rather quickly—I promise.

Most people think of themselves as truthful, but I believe you'll find that somewhere along the line you may have bought into the idea that it is better to tell a little fib than it is to be honest and possibly disappoint someone. We've taken it on ourselves to be the "feelings police," and we think we're responsible for how others respond to our honest answers. Be kind, of course, but don't be dishonest...with yourself or others.

Today I look at every option before I make a decision, and 99 percent of the time I can mentally play out the consequences of my choices in advance because I've lived long enough to have experienced most situations. Today I choose to be rigorously honest. I choose to do the right thing. And yes, even today I have to catch myself.

Now I choose to do what is best for everyone concerned,

including me, and I hold myself accountable before God for my behavior. The benefits of making good choices are mine, and I no longer suffer the consequences of making bad choices.

Once again, I go to bed happy and wake up happy. I am beyond bad choices of the type that keep me a prisoner of my mind and cause my self-talk to be scathing epistles about how worthless and disgusting I am. I am no longer making choices that keep me cowered in shame and feeling unworthy to be in relationship with God. I know in my heart those bad choices will not return. I know how to live my life purposely for Him by being available, willing, and obedient. I also know that I have to be on constant guard not to fall prey to the enemy who prowls to and fro across the earth. I have to put on the armor of God each and every day to stay strong for my King.

It is ONLY because of Jesus and the power of the Holy Spirit living within me that any of this is possible. "I have been crucified with Christ; and it is no longer I who live, but Christ lives in me; and the life which I now live in the flesh I live by faith in the Son of God, Who loved me and gave Himself up for me" (Galatians 2:20 NASB).

FALL FOR ANYTHING

It's an old saying: until you know what you stand for, you'll fall for anything. For years after I started my journey back to trusting, loving, and living for Jesus, I didn't spend any time reading His Word. I went to church and Sunday school every week. I went to fun get-togethers at the church, but I only opened my Bible in the church building. I took notes in church, marked, and underlined my Bible, and felt proud of all the pages that were showing signs that I had been there. I even put the date by the Scripture the pastor focused on that day.

I was one of those Christians who negatively influenced the people who say the church is full of hypocrites. They say they came to church, but they couldn't see that the people there led lives any different from their own, so they didn't come back. I was living in tune with the world during the week and being "good" on Sunday morning. I'm sorry I was that person, but I was where I needed to be. I was doing that one thing I know God prompted me to do. I needed to be there!

Even though it was a slow, slow, slow way to learn, the Word was being spoken, and I was able to hear enough for it to penetrate my thoughts. Eventually, that Word penetrated my heart. I repented, and I was drawn back to my Father, back to His love. I knew I truly had died and it was Christ living in me that made it possible for me to change my behavior.

For all those years, I only knew as much about the Bible as my preacher or Sunday school teacher could tell me at church. I had no idea if what they were telling me was true, if their take on what the Bible said was accurate—fact-based or opinion-based.

My Bible knowledge—the knowledge I had about what God said and what He wanted of me—was totally predicated on what someone else thought or believed. If my preacher had told me that in order for Jesus to come into my heart I'd have to travel from Dallas to Ft. Worth by ox cart and do good deeds for ten people on the way, I would have had to take his word for it. Who was I to question my pastor? I'll tell you who I am to question— I'm the only one accountable to God for my actions! So it is my business to know what God has to say about everything!

Sometimes we forget that preachers are people. I believe they do their best and because I read it in the Bible, I happen to know God holds preachers and teachers of His Word to a much higher standard of accountability than He does the rest of us. God holds them to that higher standard because He knows they are limited by their humanness, just as we are.

We are never going to BE all God has for us if we do not PERSONALLY KNOW HIS WORD. God speaks to us very intimately, and very individually, throughout His Word. If every crack of your Bible is instigated by a planned-out Bible study, you are being fed and led by someone other than the Holy Spirit as you study.

I believe some of those Bible studies are fantastic. I believe God anoints Bible study leaders too. I even believe the Holy Spirit can lead you to a specific Bible study. But until you read your Bible on your own, you will never understand that God's Word was written for you! He wrote it for YOU! He wrote it for ME! He hears and responds to our individual prayers. He wrote His Word to speak to YOU individually as you read.

For some time now I have closed my correspondence with this salutation: *Because He Lives!* (Acts 4:13).

The "Because He Lives" part is very personal to me. At times when I was overwhelmed by the messiness of my life, I felt like I didn't want to live. When I heard Gloria and Bill Gaither's song "Because He Lives," it reflected my sentiments about Jesus exactly and I have claimed it as "my" song. The chorus is the first thing that comes to mind when I am facing any hardship or feeling gratitude for my Lord.

I claimed Acts 4:13 as my life verse when I was reading through my Bible in a year. This verse convicted and convinced me to spend time with Jesus by studying and learning God's Word.

Acts 4:13 reads: "When they saw the courage of Peter and John and realized they were unschooled, ordinary men, they were astonished and took note that these men had been with Jesus" (NIV).

I had prayed many times for God's wisdom and the power to carry it out. I prayed constantly to be bold in my witness, and yet I remained painfully aware that I didn't know God's Word. What parts of His Word I did know, I didn't feel confident enough to discuss. As I read Acts 4:13, I knew the answer to wisdom was in spending time with Jesus. Though I have read the Bible through and studied much of it deeply, I am still common and uneducated. However, I know the King of kings personally, and He imparts His knowledge to me through the Holy Spirit, just as He imparted His wisdom to Peter while Peter was speaking to the Sanhedrin.

Spending time with Jesus goes well beyond reading the Bible. It includes prayer time—listening and interceding, conversing, questioning, repenting, praising, and worshiping Him.

Seeking His presence, being still enough to "know" Him and available enough to hear my name when He calls for me, is the key to maintaining contentment and joy, peace and serenity, love, patience, and kindness. My faithfulness to Him has come in fits and starts. He wants me and loves me anyway.

My self-control is still a struggle, but I noticed in His Word that *self-control* is last on the list of the fruit of the Spirit (Galatians 5:22). I figure there's a reason for that, and I continue to pick myself up when I've fallen short and begin anew without the old cat-o'-nine-tails whipping I used to give myself. Instead, I begin with sincere repentance toward my King and Savior and a desire to move ahead toward more of what He has in store for me.

The Cabin

I've briefly mentioned the "cabin" a few times and I want to bring it up again because I fully expect that I'll be having many more "cabin experiences" through the years. I don't want to give anyone the impression that "I have it made," since I know God is going to continue to mold me and grow me into the likeness of Jesus Christ—and that requires my cooperation. Humans are famous for changing their minds, forgetting, becoming willful, fostering doubt, and any number of things that make us feel separated from God, even though He is right there with us every step of the way.

For all the years I worked with Dad on his books, I assumed I would quit editing and writing for him when he quit speaking and writing. After years of pressing deadlines and working through holidays, I anticipated being the "Super Mammaw" I mentioned in chapter 2.

I fantasized about having all of our grandchildren come stay with us in waves—the first wave of the summer would bring the two oldest, then the next two, and so on until I'd gotten to take all twelve of them hiking in the LBJ National Grasslands just up the road, swimming in our favorite spring-fed stock pond, bike riding through the quiet streets of our cozy little town, and horseback riding on our acreage.

We'd walk to the donut shop in the morning and get ice cream on a stick at Roy King's feed store in the afternoon. I even imagined campouts on cool fall weekends and huge family vacations on faraway beaches. I was destined to be the most entertaining, most fun and exciting grandmother in all the land.

However, I knew my father would never retire on purpose. He often said he wasn't going to let up, give up, or shut up until he was taken up. Daddy told me shortly after his eightieth birthday that he was looking forward to cutting back on the number of speaking engagements he accepted so he could spend more time at home with Mom and devote more time to writing his books.

I believed him and mentally prepared myself for a busier schedule instead of a lighter one. I prayed my health would hold up, because it was starting to look like I might be in my eighties before I had a good chance of seriously hanging out with the grandchildren.

After Dad's fall I got busier than ever traveling with him,

interviewing him on the stage, and helping him write his books. During the four years I helped Dad onstage I started getting speaking engagements myself. When it began to look like Dad was close to giving up his speaking career, I realized that my plan of quitting when Dad quit wasn't in the cards anymore. Completely forgetting that I had told God in Columbus, Ohio, that I would go where He sent me, I suddenly felt that my life had taken off without me. That I hadn't had any real say in what was happening...it just happened. As my eyes turned away from Jesus and onto me, I became positive I was miserable once again.

So I sought help from Eunice Eastman, my treasured mentor and sister in Christ who counseled me. Eunice prescribed a cabin getaway where I could seek God's will without interruption. My cabin experience reminded me of how Jacob, in Genesis 32:24–30, wrestled with "a man" all night long. Jacob said he wouldn't stop until the man blessed him. The man turned out to be God, and God, impressed with Jacob's determination, blessed him.

We didn't wrestle outright like God did with Jacob, but He and I had a frank discussion about how I worked so much I seldom got to see my grandchildren. I blubbered to God that I was going to miss my one horseback getaway I planned every year with girlfriends, and that I wasn't going to get to go to the Gaither Family Fest in the Smokies, either. I told Him I never even considered a life of weekly travel. Didn't He KNOW that I'm a homebody?

He reminded me of Moses and the seventy elders He enlisted to help bear Moses' burden. He showed me His provision in the past and assured me of His continued provision in the future. His Word comforted and encouraged me. The tears dried and my poor-me tantrum lost its steam.

In the end I was exhausted but fine. I accepted that God had His plan, and that His plan would always be my plan too. Eventually, I remembered that my life isn't any of my business. I apologized for trying to run the show and gave it all back to Him, again.

I went home with peace and joy in my heart. Then the blessings began. Sometimes I wonder if God was just checking to see if I really meant it when I said "Send me!" After I agreed to the way God was unfolding the plan, He went and changed it...to something even better than I could fathom. God IS good! One day I really will just trust Him right from the start, even when it looks like His plan might be questionable.

JUST EXACTLY WHO IS THE "RIGHT KIND" OF PERSON?

One objective of this book is to show the blessing of transparency—living out who you truly are, allowing people to know you at an intimate level, and learning how to love others and appreciate all that went into shaping them to be the people they are today. It's about life on life's terms, how huge God is, and how women minister to one another.

A woman may desire a closer walk with Jesus—possibly the kind of walk she's admired in a more mature Christian woman she knows. But she doesn't know enough of what her Bible says to begin to know what God wants for her, what He expects from her, or even what He can empower her to do once she has fully surrendered to Him and has a heart for pleasing Him above all others, even herself. She can't get relief from her choices, past or present, because she hasn't yet discovered what God has already revealed in His Holy Word about His will for her life.

This book is about shredding that veil of false pretense and learning how to live comfortably in your own skin because Jesus loves you right where you are. This book is a call to get real and get right with God and the people with whom we share our lives. It's about real life in the trenches, "unspeakable" sins, and the sickness that engulfs those who live with secrets.

For the Christian who has cleaned up her life but shame-fully hides her past, I want her to know that she lives in bondage still. If women hide their wrongs, they are not free to help other women find a way out. There is no counsel like the counsel of one who has walked your path.

Unfortunately, Christian women—more than any other group I know—hide the truth of God's forgiveness because of shame they shouldn't even have in their lives anymore. The answer is gut-wrenching repentance, getting past shame, guilt, remorse, and regret and using your hellish past and experiences, your strength and hope, to glorify God and comfort others.

Even some Christians who have strong walks but haven't made the bad choices I've made have trouble not judging me because they can't imagine aborting a baby, being a drunk, getting a divorce, etc. The judgment of others has no ill effect on me because I am wildly, unimaginably free in Christ! I want women to "get" that for themselves. I have prayed as earnestly as I can pray for God to give me the words that will prompt women to let go and finally give their lives over to Jesus, resting in His arms...to just BE and know they're safe, and whole, and loved.

So what have I learned about who is the right kind of person? The right kind of person is the one who has grown to understand what God expects, and wants what God wants more than what they want. Becoming that person is a process, not an event. It is never too late to start becoming the person God always intended for you to be.

God bless you. I pray this book has been a source of encouragement that has helped you refocus, refuel, and rejoice in the Lord.

Because He lives!

THE CHALLENGE LIST

Did you recognize yourself somewhere within these pages? Are you tired of feeling obligated, then resentful, and ultimately violated by your own choices? Are you searching for a life of emotional stability that allows joy in the midst of your toughest trials? Hope in your darkest hour? Faith when no solution is in sight? Do you want to live for Jesus and be available, willing, and obedient to do what He has put before you to do? If so, I have a short challenge list for you.

1. If you don't have an intimate church home, find one. Fellowship is central to Christianity. We are made to be interdependent, not independent. Jesus told us to worship together because we need each other. We learn from the example of more mature Christians, and we need the accountability that fellowship affords.

2. Commit to reading the whole Bible yearly and know that it is easily done by reading the Bible daily. It is virtually impossible to live a life that is pleasing to God if you don't know what He says about how you are to live. Allow time

to study the topics that grab your heart and mind. A good study Bible is a must. The New American Standard Bible is recognized by theologians to be the closest translation of the original text. I personally enjoy my New King James Version Study Bible, but I often compare verses I'm having trouble understanding to fifteen other translations by going to Biblos at www.bible.cc and typing in the reference. Life is not frustrating when you can go to the Instruction Manual and find out how to handle every situation.

3. Commit to praying daily for godly wisdom, the truth you need to see, and the power to carry it out. Prayer is our line of direct communication with God. Talking with Him should be as second nature as talking with your best friend, mother, or spouse. A running conversation throughout the day is possible and desirable, and it helps keep life in the proper perspective.

4. Be willing to let God change you from the inside out— even if it hurts. God has a way of shining His light on the things that keep us out of relationship with Him. He allows most of us to deal with big, hard things, one at a time—in most cases. The prompting will come, the opportunity to change directions will come, and the question is, are you ready? Will you be obedient?

5. Examine your Christian walk, examine your heart, and know once and for all if you have surrendered and given

authority to Jesus Christ. If there is a chance that you've been living as a Christian by family association (your parents took you to church so you believe you are a Christian), or that you do believe in Jesus but you live with one foot in the world and one foot in church, get right with your Maker. God can get you through the hard times. He already has it handled. You can be so much more when you are His.

6. If you are stuck feeling unworthy of Christ's forgiveness even though you intellectually "know" you've been forgiven, get help now. The enemy has you bound and gagged. You need help. Get it. Your pastor, your church body, a Christian friend, a pregnancy resource center, and any other resource God has already made provision for you to use are available to you if you seek them out.

As you consider this challenge, please remember the person God made you to be. "For God did not give us a spirit of timidity, but a spirit of power, of love and of self-discipline" (2 Timothy 1:7 NIV), and "Have I not commanded you? Be strong and courageous. Do not be frightened, and do not be dismayed, for the LORD your God is with you wherever you go" (Joshua 1:9 ESV).

Get big, get bold, grab hold of that rope and start jerking and pulling your life into alignment with what God has for you. Only you can change the choices you are making. Only you can choose to be willing, available, and obedient.

Choose Jesus and be free.

ACKNOWLEDGMENTS

I owe so many so much! I pray I didn't leave out anyone who has helped shape this work in any way, but if I did please know it was simply an oversight.

My family and friends have been a tremendous support, and their efforts on my behalf have resulted in many "grati-tears" of joy and appreciation.

Thank you each and every one!

...to God, for guiding me and showing me that it is Your power by which seemingly impossible tasks are completed, and it is by Your hand that I was delivered.

...to Jim, my husband of twenty-eight years, who read every word I wrote and pushed me to explore more deeply the issues that would have been easy to bypass. Thank you for always wanting the best for me. I adore you and our life together, and I love being married to a man who loves Jesus so much.

...to my living children, DeDe, Jim, Jenni, and Amey for being the most loving, kind, thoughtful, generous, precious children in the world. God is so good to have blessed me with each one of you, and I am so proud you are mine.

...to my children in heaven, Winnie Beth Norman and Robert Curtis Norman, my heart grieves and my arms ache for you. I love and miss you with every fiber of my being and I can't wait to hold you in heaven.

...to my grandchildren, Kristina and her husband, Aaron Schrag, Desireè Galindo, Jake Norman, Sam Galindo, Parker Norman, Robert Galindo, Mable Haecker, Molly Haecker, Benjamin Fair, Averic Fair, Deacon Fair, and Phoebe Fair, God has blessed me beyond my wildest imagination with all twelve of you! I am smitten, and you have my heart from here to eternity!

...to my parents, Jean and Zig Ziglar, for always loving me and being supportive of me in every way possible. I wish everyone had parents just like you. I know I am blessed, and I pray that I honor you in all that I do.

...to my sister Cindy and brother Tom, for being wonderful siblings and for the love I always feel from you. It's nice to know somebody is always pulling for me.

...to Laurie Magers, my friend and coworker for over two decades. I would never have learned the ins-and-outs of writing and editing books without your help. Thank you for helping me edit this book and for your endless encouragement.

...to Eunice Eastman for being my sister friend in Christ as well as my wonderful mentor and counselor. You walked me through my deepest sadness back to a life of joy and intimacy with God.

...to Pastor Randy Snyder, associate pastor and counselor Ken Bryant, and the body of Christ at Highland Meadows Christian Church, who came together to help us save our marriage all those years ago, our family "is" because of your selfless help.

...to Tutti Bowles, for being my friend my whole life! Your precious, sweet spirit and willingness to love me always make me weep with gratitude for such a friend as you. Thank you for marrying Alden and sharing him with all of us. The way he loves you, Mom, Dad, and all of us is amazing!

...to Paula Reed, my friend of thirty-plus years, for loving me and always being willing to help when I need help. Your talent as a stylist has helped me shine in ways I never dreamed possible.

...to my long-time friend Marilyn Henderson for seeing what I could not see and telling me what was to come. Your heads-up allowed me to see God's hand at work in a way I might have missed otherwise.

...to my horseback riding girlfriends, Lynne Tracy, Mary LaCoste, Susie Shauf, and Beth Smith, who put up with me being out of the saddle while this work was being done. Our trail rides keep me grounded and having fun, our talks keep me sane. Also, a special thanks to Susie Shauf for the gift of copy editing the galley for me. Your efforts made a positive difference, and I'm so glad you still want to be my friend.

...to Diane Dean—first you shared your horse with me, then you shared your heart. I thank God you know a beautiful Thoroughbred when you see one and that Candy Man's soft, kind eye led to our amazing friendship.

...to Mary Michel, who ministers to my heart and soul, and to the hearts and souls of countless women in need, with her abundant love, encouragement, and prayers. God is using you in mighty ways, and I am blessed to call you friend.

...to Jan Zblewski, I thank you for your zest for life, your ability to love deeply, for sharing precious tears of mourning for your beloved Allan, for the hold-onto-your-sides, laugh-until-you-cry silliness. You crack me up every time we talk. You are 100 percent genuine, and I am your biggest fan.

...to Denise Taylor. Thank you for being my constant contact during the writing of this book. I had no idea that through you God was preparing me to deal with my granddaughter Phoebe Fair's brain cancer. I thank Him that our friendship grew instantaneously into one of complete trust and love. You bless me.

...to Pastor Gene Smith, Wren Winfield, Dianne Waggoner, Amber Roberts, Rashmi Malhotra, Beth Chapman, Kathleen Ronald, Emmy Mobley, Hollie Carron, Vicki Hitzges, Catherine Vu, Kay Brooks, Rod Brandt, Debra Pope, Krish Dhanam, Kym Glass, Elaine and Bernie Lofchick, Angie and Tommy Strader, Wendy and Andy Hansen, Sally and Phil Watts, Ching and Steve Levey, the Tonya and Todd Fenwick family, Leslie and Tim Francis, the Tyra and Michael Shannon family, Paula and Brad Ough, Michelle Prince, Suzanne Maurer, Diane Cunningham, Nicki Keohohou, Patti Smith, Kimbra Moer, Gay Adams, Kim and Alex Giles, Summer Ferguson Gulliams, and Emily Weathers. You have all sown into my life, and I am grateful for your help and friendship.

...to Carlton Garborg for seeing the potential in my story and for getting Jason Rovenstine and Joanie Garborg on board with this book. All three of you have done so much to bring this book to fruition, and I will always remember what you've done.

...to Barb Lilland, my incredible editor who walked me through needed changes so gently I wasn't even traumatized. Your input has made my book so much more than it would have been without your polishing touch. You are a real pro!

...to Randy Elliott, Lindsay Stout, and Aimee Mehl. As my father says, nothing happens until somebody sells something. Thank you for the great marketing effort.

...to Guideposts for kicking off my career in the publishing world by selecting me as a winner in the 1992 Guideposts Writers Workshop contest. The wonderful training I am blessed to have received from Elizabeth and John Sherrill has served me well these past twenty years, and I'm so excited and grateful that my writing has come full circle back to Guideposts.

...to Jay Helwig, who made the suggestion that ultimately led to this very moment in time, thank you.

About the Author

JULIE ZIGLAR NORMAN is the youngest daughter of world-renowned motivational and inspirational author and speaker Zig Ziglar and his wife, Jean. Julie shared the Get Motivated platform with her legendary father for several years, appearing to over a million individuals, before becoming the dynamic, disarming, and refreshingly transparent speaker and author she is in her own right. She is as comfortable speaking to a group of twenty-five as a venue of twenty-five thousand. Her unique experience of being raised by "the motivators' motivator" has given her a perspective on life that keeps audiences laughing, crying, and taking notes.

Continuing her father's legacy of encouragement is an honor and a privilege that Julie never expected or sought, but her willingness to accept the challenge has inspired audiences in America and abroad. Her vibrant style of delivery, her honest and transparent assessment of life, and her willingness to share intimate details of personal failures as well as personal triumphs have made her a popular crowd favorite.

As her famous father once did, Julie has shared the platform with greats such as General Colin Powell, Rudy Giuliani, President George W. Bush, Laura Bush, Dr. Robert Schuller, Howard Putnam, Joe Montana, Lou Holtz, Steve Forbes, Sarah Palin, Goldie Hawn, Bill Crosby, and many others.

Julie served as her father's editor for almost twenty years and is a winner of the coveted Guideposts Writers Workshop contest. Her background in sales, business management, and the service industry, as well as her experience as a wife, mother, stepparent, and grandmother, enable her to relate well to just about everyone. Julie lives in the sleepy little town of Alvord, Texas, with her beloved husband of twenty-eight years, Jim Norman. They have four children and twelve grandchildren.

LISTEN TO JULIE'S LIFE-CHANGING AUDIO SERIES!

ॐ

BE YOUR BEST YOU

As the daughter of Zig Ziglar, America's Motivator, Julie always heard him say that to be successful you had to BE the right kind of personal. For much of her life, Julie struggled to understand the meaning of that phrase. In this powerful CD she shares two life-changing concepts that are simple but have the ability to transform your life if understood and applied.

BEAUTIFULLY RESTORED

This powerful CD is Julie Ziglar Norman's candid testimony of restoration from post-abortion trauma. Listen as Julie presents the unvarnished truth of the regret and shame shared by millions of women in American and across the world. Julie's absolute transparency will leave no one untouched and will impact the hearts and souls of all who hear how God gave her beauty for ashes.

FIND THESE GREAT OFFERINGS AND MORE AT
WWW.ZIGLARWOMEN.COM/SHOP

Ziglar Women
refocus refuel rejoice

JULIE ZIGLAR NORMAN is the founder of Ziglar Women, a ministry that empowers Christian women to refocus, refuel, and rejoice in their Christian walk.

The mission of Ziglar Women is to challenge tentative Christianity, to inspire God's people to intensify their personal relationships with Jesus Christ, and to help them become a light in the darkness for those who seek God.

Ziglar Women presents live public events featuring Julie Ziglar Norman, daughters DeDe Galindo and Amey Fair, and other dynamic Christian women speakers. Ziglar Women conferences feature powerful testimonies, biblical solutions, and truths relevant to the real-world challenges Christian women face each day. For more information, go to www.ziglarwomen.com.